Rachel
you have such
a beautiful family
Welcome

B 2020

FRESH MANNA

Reflections on the Gospels

Fresh Manna

Four Francois, reflecting on the Four Gospels, for such a time as this.

Reflections from Matthew by Byron R. Francois.

Reflections from Mark by Benjamin Francois, III

Reflections from Luke by Brennan Francois.

Reflections from John by Cedric Francois.

print ISBN: 978-1-09832-395-0

ebook ISBN: 978-1-09832-396-7

DEDICATION

This book is dedicated to all those who are called to preach or teach the Word of God as well as to anyone who recognizes their need for daily spiritual Bread. Your hunger for this Bread, your appetite for divine inspiration, is what leads to understanding the life changing, life enhancing messages contained in the Bible. Stay hungry our friends!

In addition, this book is dedicated to Stephanie Francois, Cheryl Francois and Delores Francois. These women are the wives of Benjamin, Byron and Cedric. Each of you have stood beside your husbands, prayed for them and been a major part of their inspiration through the years. This book would not have happened without each of you. Thank you for who you are and all you mean to the Francois family.

To those who supported this book with your skills or with your resources, we thank you. While we cannot record all your names, we recognize that we are stronger and more impactful because you are with us. Thank you for believing in this book and believing in the calling of God on the lives and ministry of the Francois family.

CONTENTS

FRESH MANNA
INTRODUCTION

When tempted by the devil in the wilderness Jesus quoted Scripture. It was the devil's aim to derail Jesus from His mission. The initial challenge, after going 40 days without eating food, was to get Jesus to turn stone into bread. Jesus' response to this test was from the sacred writings found in Deuteronomy 8:3,

> *"Man shall not live by bread alone but by every word that proceeds from the mouth of God" Matthew 4:4 NKJV.*

If we are to be successful in our personal walk with God, if we are to have ministries that are powerful and life changing, it is imperative that we be well nourished daily. This nourishment comes from reading, reflecting on and putting into practice the Word of God. The Word is our daily bread.

> *"Your words were found, and I ate them, and Your word was to me the joy and rejoicing of my heart;" Jeremiah 5:16 NKJV*

> *"So He humbled you, allowed you to hunger, and fed you with manna which you did not know nor did your fathers know, that He might make you know that man shall not live by bread alone; but man lives by every word that proceeds from the mouth of the LORD." Deuteronomy 8:3 NKJV*

Manna was provided daily, not just for physical nourishment, but also as a graphic reminder that the Word of God is food and fuel for our lives. *Exodus 16* shares how God's daily provision worked. Fresh manna was provided daily. Every morning manna was available to God's people. Yesterday's portion of manna would not sustain them. Each new day required a fresh serving of bread.

In a similar way, we need a fresh Word from God daily. We grow from the nutrients and energy gained from devouring our daily bread. This book, "Fresh Manna", is designed to not only give you exciting revelations from the four Canonical Gospels, but to inspire and encourage you to seek fresh manna yourself every time you open the Word of God. We believe God still communicates to and through willing human vessels. We believe He does this through ordinary people. The writers of the Gospels as well as those they wrote about were common ordinary people, like you, and the Francois' who contributed to this collection of reflections. God can and will speak to and through anyone who is willing to connect with God daily.

The reflections on each of the Gospels, Matthew, Mark, Luke and John are not intended to be exhaustive in scope. Our intention is not to produce a full commentary on the first four books of the New Testament. We simply desire to model the power of inspiration through reflection. Each contributor read from their assigned Gospel, reflected prayerfully on what was read, then chronicled those reflections. From this came fresh insights and understandings that enhances our personal walk with God and enriches our preaching and teaching. As you read these reflections, you may ask as did the Israelites in the wilderness, "What is it?" (See Exodus16:15). Fresh revelation at times is vastly different from the traditional ways of looking at or interpreting Bible passages. Because of this, your thinking and understanding will be challenged. We encourage you to be open-minded as you read. Be willing to allow God to show you fresh insights and revelations. Be inspired. Be blessed.

It is our hope and prayer that reading "Fresh Manna" will motivate and inspire you to take God's Word, read it, reflect on it and allow God's Spirit to gracefully guide you to fresh and exciting insights that will revolutionize your walk with Him. For our colleagues in the pulpit, we pray this read will help to revitalize your preaching and teaching. Fresh manna nourished God's people on their way to the earthly Promised Land. We believe Fresh Manna will in turn; nourish you in preparation for the heavenly Promised Land.

ABOUT THE CONTRIBUTORS

BYRON R. FRANCOIS

Byron R. Francois was born and raised in New Orleans, Louisiana and graduated from McDonogh 35 College Prep High School. His undergraduate degree was earned at Oakwood College (Now Oakwood University), in Huntsville, AL where he excelled in both Biblical Greek and Hebrew. He did his graduate studies at The University of New Orleans. Byron is married to Cheryl Humphrey-Francois, MD for 33 years. They have two adult children, Lauren, a Psychologist in Dallas, TX, and Lacey a Civilian Contract Worker for the US Government at Sheppard Air Force Base in Wichita Falls, TX. Byron's ministry began in 1989. He was ordained a minister in the Seventh-day Adventist denomination in 1996. For more than 25 years, he has served as a full and part time pastor. His ministry included church districts in Louisiana, Texas and Oklahoma. Byron has a unique approach to sharing the word of God and embraces every opportunity to do so through both the spoken and written word. He is currently the Director of Services at a Christian nonprofit in Wichita Falls, Texas.

BENJAMIN FRANCOIS, III

Benjamin is from New Orleans, LA. He graduated from the first African American school in New Orleans, McDonogh 35 Sr. High School. He earned a Bachelor of Science Degree in Business Administration/Management from the University of Phoenix.

Currently, Benjamin is the Lead Pastor of the Glad Tidings SDA Church in Slidell, Louisiana. His passion for ministering to Young Adults and Children has helped the church experience significant growth.

Prior to pastoring, Benjamin retired from the State of Louisiana Department of Children and Family Services where he served as Regional Executive Director for the New Orleans Region for 25 years.

Benjamin has enjoyed a wonderful marriage of 43 years to his wife Stephanie Mathis Francois. Together they lead Family Life Seminars specializing in dating and marriage. They have two adult daughters, Jaime, who works for the Jefferson Parish School District and Erica, who serves as Social Worker. They have one son-in-law and one future son-in-law along with four beautiful granddaughters.

Benjamin is a forever native of New Orleans, LA and is the oldest of five siblings. He is fascinated with the love that Christ has for him as revealed in one of his favorite bible text, Romans 5:8, "But God commendeth His love toward us, in that, while we were yet sinners, Christ died for us."

BRENNAN FRANCOIS

Originally, from New Orleans, LA, Brennan graduated from McDonogh 35 College Prep High School in NOLA in 1976. He completed his undergraduate degree in Theology at Southwestern Adventist University in Keene, TX in 1982. He earned his Masters of Divinity from Jacksonville Theological Seminary in Jacksonville, FL in 2011. He completed four Units of Clinical Pastoral Education (CPE) at Eisenhower Army Medical Center in Ft. Gordon, GA in 2005.

Brennan, CEO of *Dynamic Living, Inc.* is the author of 2 other books, **Hannnnng in There**, and **52 Weeks of Dynamic Living.** He is the creator of the empowerment and encouragement **CD series** called **Keys to Dynamic Living.** Brennan can be seen delivering life enhancing messages at **www. brennanismad.com.**

In addition to *Dynamic Living, Inc.*, Brennan, for 25 years is serving as the Associate Director of Pastoral Care at AU Health/Augusta University in Augusta, GA. Brennan is also the Care Pastor for a church plant in Grovetown, GA called CHOSEN.

Brennan is the father of three children, Jackie, who works for La Madeline's in New Orleans, LA, Brennan Jamaal, who is a pastor and music/gospel/rap artist and Michael Dominque who works for John Deer and is a music/hip hop artist. Brennan has six precious grandchildren.

Brennan has worked as a pastor, a college and high school chaplain, a coach, and an athletic director.

CEDRIC FRANCOIS

A native of New Orleans Louisiana, Cedric was educated in the New Orleans Public School System, graduating from John F. Kennedy Sr. High School in 1975. Cedric earned a Degree in Mass Media Communications from Southwestern Adventist College in 1981 and went to work in commercial television and radio at NBC affiliate K.B.C.U TV Lubbock Texas. Cedric's long and brilliant career has afforded him the privilege of using his gifts for businesses and churches around the world as well as ministries such as "The Breath of Life" television program, Evangelist Oscar Lane Jr., the PTL satellite network, and many more. Cedric is currently the CEO of DeeCee7 Media Solutions "Media Moving Messages" and is influencing ministries and people globally.

Cedric has been married to Delores (Riley) Francois for 39 Years. They have two adult children, Joslynn an Elementary Education Administrator and Ashton a Recording Engineer and Film Industry Technician, three grandchildren, Nadia, Dee and Myles and one baby, "Sasha" their Mini Schnauzer. Whenever Cedric is not working on creating Media he is working on his golf game.

You can keep up-to-date with Cedric by several ongoing initiatives:

www.dc7media.com

vimeo.com/dc7media new.livestream.com/dc7media

youtube.com/dc7media

cfrancois@dc7media.com

504.621.9229

DC7 Media Solutions 328 Brasfield Dr. Huntsville, Alabama 35806

REFLECTIONS ON
THE BOOK OF MATTHEW

REFLECTIONS ON MATTHEW 1

WHO'S YOUR DADDY?

"The book of the generation of Jesus Christ, the son of David, the son of Abraham."

It seems unusual that Matthew would begin his gospel with a long list of names. Why Matthew would embark on such a task? They believed in the purity of one's lineage. The importance of this can be understood in the groupings of Jesus' lineage. There are three groups, each with 14 individuals. The groups are arranged in such a way that we can readily memorize them. These groups also make it clear that Jesus is from the linage of David. There is no misunderstanding this fact. New Testament writers such as Peter (***Acts 2:29-36***) and Paul (***Romans 1:3***) both speak of Jesus being a descendent of David. Repeatedly, Jesus is addressed as the Son of David in various text, ***Matthew 12:23***, ***Matthew 15:22***, ***Matthew 20:30, 31*** and ***Matthew 21:9, 15.***

We live in an era where individuals are extremely interested in their family lineage. With all of the genealogy and D.N.A. testing kits available to us, searches can lead to incredible results. However, when considering the lineage of Jesus Christ and the names on his family tree, there is no doubt that the genealogy of Jesus is accurate and factual.

These names consist of people who are from various backgrounds. It breaks down the barrier that exist between people based on race, gender; and most important of all the barrier between the saint and sinner.

"There is neither Jew nor Greek, there is neither bond nor free, there is neither male nor female: for ye are all one in Christ Jesus." Galatians 3:28

"Now the birth of Jesus Christ was on this wise: When as his mother Mary was espoused to Joseph, before they came together, she was found with child of the Holy Ghost." Matthew 1:18.

Mary who is engaged to Joseph is pregnant with a baby that was gifted to her by the Holy Ghost. There could not have been a more loving way for God to demonstrate His love and care for all of humanity in this miraculous act. Only God could have done such a thing, the progenitor of life. What a huge responsibility it must have been for both parents to raise Jesus, especially Joseph. He is called to be the father of a child that he did not have anything to do with bringing into this world. He was given the responsibility to raise Jesus. Can you imagine some of the experiences they shared during those early years and into the teen years? Think about your experiences with your dad as a young boy. Maybe Jesus shared some similar experiences that related to His day. While we all have dads, we must know who our true father is. Who's your daddy?

REFLECTIONS ON MATTHEW 2

HOW SMART ARE YOU?

"[1] Now when Jesus was born in Bethlehem of Judaea in the days of Herod the king, behold, there came wise men from the east to [9]have seen his star in the east, and are come to worship him."

The text says **"…wise men…"** went looking for the baby Jesus. The Bible, from Genesis to Revelation is a journey for wise men to search for and come to know Jesus. From the first man and woman, Adam and Eve to the Israelites experience in Egypt, man has been looking for Jesus. The prophets of old looked for Jesus. The prophets of old looked for Jesus and the apostles of the New Testament looked for this Jesus, the coming Messiah.

Why do the wise men found in the Gospel of Matthew look for Jesus? Like the wise before them, and the wise in this generation, they read the prophecies and were blessed with insight and understanding. This insight caused them to look for and follow His star. No distance prevented them from seeking and finding Jesus. They knew He was the answer to every question. He was the solution to every problem. He is air, light, water and everything we need to live now and for eternity.

Wise men today must look for Jesus also. With the many issues facing us today, from physical, mental and social health to financial concerns, we would be wise to look for Jesus. The wise will look for Jesus in every life experience, whether positive or negative. Some men do not seek Jesus because they do not believe in Him.

> *"The fool hath said in his heart, there is no God..."*
> *Psalm 14:1.*

How wise are you? Matthew tells us that when the wise men found Jesus they "*...fell down, and worshipped him..." Matthew 2:11.* Finding Jesus is like finding a treasure that cannot be quantified. Jesus is worthy of our worship and praise and once He is found by us there is nothing that can contain our worship of Him. Finding Jesus will not cause our problems and sorrows in life to disappear; but He will give us the ability to bear any and every burden that we are called to carry. Worship Jesus in all circumstances. Our circumstances do not change who Jesus is or what He can and will do on our behalf.

> *"[13]And when they were departed, behold, the angel of the Lord appeareth to Joseph in a dream, saying, Arise, and take the young child and his mother, and flee into Egypt, and be thou there until I bring thee word: for Herod will seek the young child to destroy him."*

An angel of the Lord tells Mary and Joseph to flee to Egypt with the baby Jesus. Herod angered that the wise men did not return to him with the location of the Christ child, decides to kill all of the children in Bethlehem under the age of two. This foolish ruler believes he can preserve his kingship by eliminating any potential threat to his rule. How foolish to think you are able to take the life of the one who He Himself is the giver and sustainer of life. How foolish to believe you can receive the worship that is due only to the one true King of kings and Lord of lords, Jesus. Wise men know this. How wise are you?

Just as God sustained the life of His Son Jesus, God will also sustain us. Being sustained may mean being led to a place we have never been or participating in something that we have never done. My daily prayer is for Jesus to lead me. Where He leads me I will follow. Some call that foolish, but I call it being wise. *"¹⁹ But when Herod was dead..."* Consider carefully the words of this verse, Herod dies. The Herod wished for the baby Jesus turned out to be his own undoing. Know this; what the devil intends to bring your harm is the very thing that destroys him. God promises that He will make your enemies your footstool, (*Hebrews 1:13*). Herod dies and Jesus returns to Nazareth. Herod reaches an end as Jesus begins His life and ministry.

REFLECTIONS ON MATTHEW 3

A CHURCH WITHOUT WALLS

"¹In those days came John the Baptist, preaching in the wilderness of Judaea, ²And saying, Repent ye: for the kingdom of heaven is at hand."

Preaching in the wilderness, what an unusual concept. Even during the times of Christ wilderness preaching would be uncommon. It is intriguing that John did not set up his pulpit in the city or the sanctuary of his day. Rather he found himself in the wilderness proclaiming the good news. In such a vast space his voice must have resounded over the hills and down through the valleys of the wilderness. It seems evident that John is a student of what we know now to be the Old Testament, because he has taken up the call given in **Isaiah 58:1**,

"Cry aloud, spare not, lift up thy voice like a trumpet, and shew my people their transgression, and the house of Jacob their sins."

The word of God has the power to draw men, women, boys and girls as evident by the preaching of John. Not only did people come out to the wilderness to hear him, they were beginning to confess their sins and submitted to baptism.

When we are convicted by the word of God, there is an urgency to share that word with anyone who will hear us. In John's day, there was no internet. Facebook, Twitter, Instagram and Myspace were not around to inform people that John was preaching in the wilderness. John's preaching, like a magnet, drew people. What they heard brought conviction to the soul. When they returned to their homes, they shared what they heard. This preaching was not the "pie in the sky" message many want to hear. This preaching was a denunciation of evil and sin regardless of whom the sinner was. Calling men to repentance was the theme of the message. Always be mindful that when the Word of God is proclaimed, there will be some who will come out, not to be enlightened by the word, but to be "pot stirrers," as I like to call them, those who only want to cause problems.

> "[7]But when he saw many of the Pharisees and Sadducees come to his baptism... [9] **And think not to say within yourselves, we have Abraham to our father...**[11]I indeed baptize you with water unto repentance. **But he that cometh after me is mightier than I, whose shoes I am not worthy to bear: he shall baptize you with the Holy Ghost, and with fire:** [12]Whose fan is in his hand, and he will thoroughly purge his floor, and gather his wheat into the garner; but he will burn up the chaff with unquenchable fire."

John's preaching was not an advertisement for himself. His preaching pointed to the one who was to come, Jesus. This Jesus, when he came, would baptize men with the Holy Ghost. The Holy Ghost or Holy Spirit can do so much for us, for its deepest meaning simply means breath. What is breath to us, breath is life so here we have the promise of life given to us with this baptism. Another meaning for Spirit is wind and wind denotes power. The Spirit of God therefore can be called The Power of God. With this power, we are able to do the unimaginable; we are able to bear the unbearable. With this power, we are able to do the undoable. We are unbounded with regard to what we can accomplish with The Power of God through the Holy Spirit. No one wants to be weak in any phase of his or her life. With the Holy Spirit we will never be weak for He will enable us to be as strong as steel and as rooted as deeply planted tree.

"¹³Then cometh Jesus from Galilee to Jordan unto John, to be baptized of him."

Why is Jesus being baptized? Those baptized by John prior to Jesus were confessing their sins and repenting. Jesus, according to scripture had no sins to confess and no need to repent.

Baptism was not an official part of Judaism. For Jesus to take such a bold step and allow Himself to be baptized by John in the presence of ordinary people, as well as religious leaders like the Pharisees and Sadducees, demonstrates a profound fact. The fact is that Jesus was confirming all men, Jew and non-Jew were sinners. That all needed saving and this was the way. God the Father confirms and affirms this fact in vs. 16.

"And Jesus, when he was baptized, went up straightway out of the water: and, lo, the heavens were opened unto him, and he saw the Spirit of God descending like a dove, and lighting upon him: ¹⁷And lo a voice from heaven, saying, This is my beloved Son, in whom I am well pleased."

REFLECTIONS ON MATTHEW 4

TEMPTED BY THE 3 A'S

"¹Then was Jesus led up of the Spirit into the wilderness to be tempted of the devil. ²And when he had fasted forty days and forty nights, he was afterward an hungred."

If we have not learned by now we should all know that Satan does not fight fair. His attacks on us mainly come when we are at our weakest most vulnerable moments. His temptations are fashioned in such a way that they appear tailor made just for us.

In Matthew 4 there are three temptations mentioned. The first is Appetite. Appetite is a natural desire to satisfy the bodily need for food.

"³And when the tempter came to him, he said, If thou be the Son of God, command that these stones be made bread."

Satan has always used appetite as a primary way to get us to fall and fail. If we have difficulty controlling what goes into our mouths we will have difficulty controlling what comes out of it. In addition to this, an uncontrollable appetite increases the risks health issues. Many times these problems become too much to overcome. Satan attempts to call into question who Jesus is by saying, *"…if thou be the Son of God…"* Without question, Satan knew who Jesus was. More importantly Jesus knew who He was and whose He was. We must have that same assurance. When we know who we are and whose we are, we are empowered to be overcomers. Only when we forget our identity that do we stand in jeopardy of falling.

Then the devil attempts to tell Jesus what to do, **"…command that these stones be made bread."** You can't tell Jesus what to do. There was no way Satan could command Jesus to do anything, Jesus is the commander. Because Jesus was physically hungry from fasting forty days Satan assumed He would take the bait. He was confident Jesus would feed Himself. Remember, Jesus knows who He is. He knows He is not in this for Himself. Jesus is in this for you and me. Selfishness would have dictated that the stones be made bread and Jesus would eat. However, love dictated that the stones remain stones. The word of God would be more than enough to sustain Him through this temptation.

Stones turned to bread would not have cured the hunger of Christ. His fasting was not for weight loss or for any health concern. No, He hungered for sinful souls. He hungered for the sick and the lame. He hungered for the unbelieving. He hungered for the outcast souls. He hungered for humanity. His fasting was for the ministry that lay ahead of Him to be the one who would take away the sins of the world.

> *"⁴But he answered and said, It is written, Man shall not live by bread alone, but by every word that proceedeth out of the mouth of God."*

The second temptation is assumption. Assumption simply means to take for granted that something will happen.

> *"⁵Then the devil taketh him up into the holy city, and setteth him on a pinnacle of the temple, ⁶And saith unto him, **If thou be the Son of God, cast thyself down: for it is written, He shall give his angels charge concerning thee: and in their hands they shall bear thee up, lest at any time thou dash thy foot against a stone**."*

As a young boy I always thought that I needed to have a near death experience in order to know who Jesus was and for Him to show me what He could do. One evening I was playing in an open field near some train tracks with my cousin. I decided that when I heard the train coming I would run alongside of the train and jump in front of it; and if Jesus was real He would allow me to beat the train across and I would live and tell a powerful story in church that coming weekend. It was going to be a powerful story because I had a witness. As the train approached, I begin to run and at the precise moment I was to jump in front of the train, I fell down. The train passed and my powerful testimony was ruined. I asked my cousin if I had been running fast, his response was "absolutely not". He then stated it was a good thing I fell down because I was not going to make it. We can never assume upon the goodness of Christ. Satan underestimates the resolve of Christ. We never have to put ourselves in a position to force God to do something to prove Himself. God does not need testing; He has a proven track record as to what He can do on our behalf.

> *"⁷Jesus said unto him, It is written again, Thou shalt not tempt the Lord thy God."*

The third temptation is authority. Authority is the power or right to give orders, make decisions, and enforce obedience.

> *"⁸Again, the devil taketh him up into an exceeding high mountain, and sheweth him all the kingdoms of the world, and the glory of them; ⁹And saith unto him, All these things will I give thee,* if thou wilt fall down and worship me." You cannot give anyone something they already possess. Jesus has full authority over the kingdoms of the world. Because of this fact Jesus is the only one who commands our worship. It is amazing how Satan appears to have forgotten that God created him and if anyone is going to do any bowing down it will be him. *"That at the name of Jesus every knee should bow, of things in heaven, and things in earth, and things under the earth…" Philippians 2:10.*

When the Bible says every knee shall bow, it includes all people, everyone without exception.

"¹⁰Then saith Jesus unto him, Get thee hence, Satan: for it is written, Thou shalt worship the Lord thy God, and him only shalt thou serve.¹¹ Then the devil leaveth him, and, behold, angels came and ministered unto him."

Jesus tells him to "…get out of His sight, just go away…" and just like that Satan left Him alone and was gone. We must exercise that same authority. When Satan gets into our personal space, tell him to get out of your face and he will be gone.

"¹⁸And Jesus, walking by the sea of Galilee, saw two brethren, Simon called Peter, and Andrew his brother, casting a net into the sea: for they were fishers.¹⁹And he saith unto them, Follow me, and I will make you fishers of men. ²⁰And they straight-way left their nets, and followed him. ²¹And going on from thence, he saw other two brethren, James the son of Zebedee, and John his brother, in a ship with Zebedee their father, mending their nets; and he called them. ²²And they immediately left the ship and their father, and followed him."

Do you ever reflect back to the time where you first encountered Jesus? Can you remember the circumstances surrounding that encounter? What exactly where you doing? It does not matter where Jesus encounters us. Jesus calls us to follow Him and be a co-worker with Him. As we follow Jesus, we will find ourselves going uptown and downtown. Crossing railroad tracks and overpasses. Entering gated communities and housing developments. We are responding to the call to follow Christ and do as He commands.

What did Jesus do as He went about? He went out and met the needs of the people, mainly through healing. He cured their physical and mental afflictions. As His name begins to circulate around the region, people came from all over to be healed of their infirmities. What a blessing it is to know that Jesus not only preached the gospel in word but He preached the gospel in action. You may remember this popular saying, "What Would Jesus Do" The question that should truly get us motivated is "What Did Jesus Do"

"And Jesus went about all Galilee, teaching in their synagogues, and preaching the gospel of the kingdom, and healing all manner of sickness and all manner of disease among the people." Matthew 4:23.

REFLECTIONS ON MATTHEW 5

SHOUT IT FROM THE MOUNTAINTOP

We meet people daily who use these phrase, "Be blessed", "Have a blessed day" and "I'm blessed". If we truly want to be blessed and have a blessed day, it is outlined for us in the beginning of Matthew 5.

*"³**Blessed are the poor in spirit**: for theirs is the kingdom of heaven. ⁴**Blessed are they that mourn**: for they shall be comforted. ⁵**Blessed are the meek**: for they shall inherit the earth. 6 **Blessed are they which do hunger and thirst after righteousness**: for they shall be filled. ⁷**Blessed are the merciful**: for they shall obtain mercy. ⁸**Blessed are the pure in hear**t: for they shall see God. ⁹**Blessed are the peacemakers**: for they shall be called the children of God. ¹⁰**Blessed are they which are persecuted for righteousness' sake**: for theirs is the kingdom of heaven. ¹¹**Blessed are ye, when men shall revile you, and persecute you, and shall say all manner of evil against you falsely, for my sake.***

¹²Rejoice, and be exceeding glad: for great is your reward in heaven: for so persecuted they the prophets which were before you." The text tells us that there are benefits given to those who are blessed. How encouraging it should be to us to know that God Himself has bestowed His divine favor on us. Shout it from the mountaintop, I am blessed by God!

*"¹³**Ye are the salt of the earth**: but if the salt have lost his savour, wherewith shall it be salted? it is thenceforth good for nothing, but to be cast out, and to be trodden under foot of men."*

Salt is perhaps most well known as a food preservative and flavoring agent. Salt plays a crucial role in maintaining human health. It is the main source of sodium and chloride ions in the human diet. Sodium is essential for nerve and muscle function and is involved in the regulation of fluids in the body. Sodium also plays a role in the body's control of blood pressure and volume. Jesus says that we are ***"…the salt of the earth…"***

Before there were refrigerators and freezers, salt was essential for preserving food, keeping it from going bad. We are in this world not only to preserve it but also to keep it from going bad. We must be salt in the home, salt on the job, salt at the church, salt at the mall, salt at the convenience store, you get the point. Salt has a way of lending its flavor to that which it is placed upon. We must lend our flavor those we encounter. We will then experience a change in our homes, communities, work places and places of worship.

> "[14]***Ye are the light of the world****. A city that is set on an hill cannot be hid.* [15]*Neither do men light a candle, and put it under a bushel, but on a candlestick; and it giveth light unto all that are in the house.* [16]*Let your light so shine before men, that they may see your good works, and glorify your Father which is in heaven."*

There are many uses for light; the main purpose is so that we would not be darkness. We are to be the light of the world so that the world would not be in darkness. The darkness I am speaking of is spiritual darkness. Our lights are to shine on those who are in spiritual darkness. We should be a light to the lonely soul. We should be a light to the weary soul. We should be a light to the hungry soul. We should be a light to those who are less fortunate. There different types of lights. We have to decide what type of light we want to be. We do not want to be a match light. Match lights burn but only for a short period and then they go out. We do not want to be like a flashlight. Flashlights burn as long as they have a source of ignition like batteries, but when the batteries fail, the flashlight goes out. We do not want to be like a headlight. Headlights glow for far distances but they like flashlights must also have a source of ignition like batteries and if not, headlights fail. The word used for light is the Greek word **"lampw"** (lampo) – which means to be a piercing beam, shine like a torch, and radiate brilliancy. Always remember, while our lights are shining brightly, they shine for the glory of God and God alone.

"²¹Ye have heard that it was said of them of old time, Thou shalt not kill; and whosoever shall kill shall be in danger of the judgment:"

We all have been angry at some point in our lives. Holding on to anger is like holding on to a burning rock; the only person who gets hurt is the one with the rock in his hand. Put the burning rock down.

"²³Therefore if thou bring thy gift to the altar, and there rememberest that thy brother hath ought against thee; ²⁴Leave there thy gift before the altar, and go thy way; first be reconciled to thy brother, and then come and offer thy gift."

Some people often believe that they can go through the motions of church rituals, praying, and singing, giving of tithes and offering and feel as if they have come close to Christ. However, if those things are done with ill will towards their brother or sister it is of no consequence. It does not make us any less a Christian, man, or woman to go to someone we have wronged or who has wronged us and sincerely say that we are sorry. We can never be right with God unless we are right with our fellow man. We must reconcile with our family members, our co-workers, our neighbors, our friends and even those strangers we may have encountered if we want to see Jesus in peace.

"²⁷Ye have heard that it was said by them of old time, Thou shalt not commit adultery:"

We have heard the saying that **"…you can look but don't touch…"** Some have come to believe that this is an acceptable practice in society. It is not an acceptable practice to look and not touch. This text admonishes us to avoid even the simplest forms of adultery. While it is challenging to keep ourselves under physical, mental, and social control, we must do whatever it takes to subdue those things that may cause us problems. We should not allow anything to cause us to miss out on our ultimate blessing and that is being saved in Gods kingdom.

"³¹It hath been said, Whosoever shall put away his wife, let him give her a writing of divorcement."

I have been married for over 30 plus years and have never thought about giving my wife a document stating that I want a divorce. In times of old this was a common practice because women were viewed as objects as opposed to equal partners in a relationship. The easy way out of a situation is not always the best way. Remember there are consequences to every action we perform.

> "³³Again, ye have heard that it hath been said by them of old time, Thou shalt not forswear thyself, but shalt perform unto the Lord thine oaths: ³⁴But I say unto you, Swear not at all; neither by heaven; for it is God's throne: ³⁵Nor by the earth; for it is his footstool: neither by Jerusalem; for it is the city of the great King. ³⁶Neither shalt thou swear by thy head, because thou canst not make one hair white or black. ³⁷But let your communication be, Yea, yea; Nay, nay: for whatsoever is more than these cometh of evil."

What is an oath? An oath is either a statement of fact or a promise with wording relating to something considered sacred as a sign of verity. We have heard the saying **"…my word is my bond…"**

When I was in elementary school, I would often hear other kids say things like, **"…I swear on my mother's grave…"** and **"…I swear to god…"** This would allegedly give some validity to whatever they were swearing to. Swearing seems to imply that a person is attempting to prove something and often times swearing by something or making an oath does not make that something true.

> "³⁸Ye have heard that it hath been said, An eye for an eye, and a tooth for a tooth:"

It is so easy to want to get back at those who may have harmed us in any way. Is it difficult to love our enemies? Is it difficult to love those that curse us? Is it difficult to love those that despise and use us? Is it difficult to love those who hate us? The answer is yes, but it is not impossible to do. There are three basic Greek words for love. The first is **agaph** (agape), used to describe the highest form of love (God's love for man). Second is **filew** (phileo), which is commonly used to describe as love between friends. And the third is **eros** (eros), which is used to describe as the physical, sensual intimacy between a husband and wife. The word used in this text is **"agaph"** (agape). We are to love those who appear unlovable with the same love that God demonstrates towards us. This takes some doing. Loving the unlovable is a character trait that can and will benefit us.

Matthew 5 concludes with these words,

> *"Be ye therefore perfect, even as your Father which is in heaven is perfect."*

Can we be "perfect" like God? This is a challenging question to answer. The context of text implies that we are to be mature and complete with regard to our treatment of others. We are to love others and do all that we can to imitate the character of God. Can we truly be perfect like God? We can be perfect like our heavenly father by demonstrating a type of love for our fellow man that never wavers, even in the face of being mistreated.

Let's not get caught up in attempting to do everything right and saying all the right words. It would be extremely stressful to go each day trying not to make a mistake. When we learn to forgive as God forgives and to love as God loves this will allow us to be on the path to Christian perfection.

REFLECTIONS ON MATTHEW 6

WALK IT LIKE YOU TALK IT

> *"[1] Take heed that ye do not your alms before men, to be seen of them: otherwise ye have no reward of your Father which is in heaven. [2] Therefore when thou doest thine alms, do not sound a trumpet before thee, as the hypocrites do in the synagogues and in the streets, that they may have glory of men. Verily I say unto you, They have their reward. [3] But when thou doest alms, let not thy left hand know what thy right hand doeth: 4 That thine alms may be in secret: and thy Father which seeth in secret himself shall reward thee openly."*

Who does not like to be seen, especially when they are doing something very big and important? Often we do things to seek the approval or accolades of men and women. We all have witnessed individuals with signs that read, "Will work for food" or "Need money for rent" etc. When we give money to the ones holding such signs, we cannot wait to tell someone the good deed we've done. Jesus tells us to do for others but not to draw any attention to ourselves. This can also apply to our giving in our respective houses of worship. There is no prize given to the one who gives the most but rather to one who gives honestly and consistently.

Jesus lays out the foundation of our prayers and does not mince words in **verses 5-15**. Often when we think of Jesus, we do not envision Him speaking harshly and direct to people. Jesus uses words like "hypocrite" describing a person who pretends to have certain beliefs, attitudes or feelings when they really do not; those who say one thing and do another; those who like to be seen and heard while praying. He also uses the word "heathen" denoting a person who does not belong to a widely held religion.

Have you ever attended a church gathering or special religious service that is well attended? If so, you may have been present to experience a long drawn out prayer. At times, the bigger the turn out for worship meant the longer the prayer would be for the service. Our prayers should not be formalized prayers with a standardized or repetitive tone. These types of prayers can become meaningless and ineffective. Think about the prayer you offer when blessing your meanls. "Lord we thank you for the food that we are about to receive for the nourishment of our bodies, for Christ sake, amen." If that sounds familiar to you, you may want to rethink your prayer of thanks for your meal. Our prayers should always begin with acknowledging the true and living God. We should pray for what we need, not what we want. There is a huge difference from our needs and wants. We should always ask God to forgive of our sins. As God forgives us we learn how to forgive those who have wronged us in any way.

We can see in the later part of **Matthew 6** how God takes care of our needs on a very personal level. Nature proves to be an excellent example of how God provides for His creation. From feeding the birds to keeping the flowers growing in season, God knows how to take care of us. There is never any need to look to anyone or anything else. In life, we worry and are concerned about many things. While some things are more important than others are, we all have our stress points.

At the time of this writing, we have two dogs in our home, Max and Ruby. I have never seen them stress about what they are going to eat or where they are going to sleep. Every day we give them various treats and snacks. Their dinners are filled with roasted chicken and turkey mixed with dog food. They sleep very well on the leather couches and look extremely healthy and happy. When God is first in our lives, we should have no worries about anything.

"And my God will liberally supply (fill until full) your every need according to His riches in glory in Christ Jesus." Philippians 4:19, Amplified Bible.

REFLECTIONS ON MATTHEW 7

THE JURY FINDS YOU GUILTY

"Judge not, that ye be not judged." Matthew 7:1

Christians can be very judgmental of individuals who may not believe as they do. Many professed Christians are quick to point out the problems with the entire world and not be aware of their own issues. It is easy to be judgmental because we just find the person who is just a little less than we are and we have an easy mark. It is easy to judge the man with $5 when we have $10. It is easy to judge the unemployed person when we have a job. It is easy to judge the person who does not smell good when we have had a shower. It is easy to judge the person at the bus stop when we are driving. It is easy to judge the smoker when we do not smoke. It is easy to judge the one who drinks alcohol when we do not drink. However, while all of this judging is going on, who is judging us? We must make every effort to work on ourselves first before we start to look at someone else's situation. None of us is in any position to judge anyone. Remember, we are not judged by a jury of our peers; we are judged by God.

What gives God the authority to judge us? What gives God the authority to be both the judge and the jury? God is righteous.

"And the heavens shall declare his righteousness: for God is judge himself." Psalm 50:6.

Our eternal lives are at stake. We can ill afford to be found guilty. Life is full of choices and how we choose to live and navigate this life will determine our final verdict. Some individuals want to take the easy way and any shortcut they can find. Keep in mind when navigating life that it is not a sprint, rather it is a marathon.

Our lives must exemplify who Christ is in both word and actions. While on occasions we can fool man, we cannot fool God. God does not judge us by our looks nor by type of vehicle we drive or the size of our home. God judges the heart.

"...for man looketh on the outward appearance, but the Lord looketh on the heart." 1 Samuel 16:7.

The jury finds you guilty! Who wants this to be the last thing they hear?

REFLECTIONS ON MATTHEW 8

I HAVE NO INSURANCE

"⁴Surely he hath borne our griefs, and carried our sorrows: yet we did esteem him stricken, smitten of God, and afflicted. ⁵But he was wounded for our transgressions, he was bruised for our iniquities: the chastisement of our peace was upon him; and with his stripes we are healed." Isaiah 53:4, 5.

If you have ever been to the doctor's office for an appointment you are greeted with these words, "do you have your insurance card"? In some cases, if you do not have insurance you will not be able to make an appointment. Insurance provides financial coverage for unforeseen circumstances surrounding various situations that may arise in our lives. Insurance provides a guarantee of compensation for specified loss, damage or illness. It is challenging to manage without insurance.

Matthew 8 has several miraculous healings by Jesus provided to individuals who did not have any insurance. The leper surely did not have any insurance. The captain's servant did not have any insurance. Peter's mother in law did not have any insurance. They had no means to go to the local physician and seek medical attention. Unknown to them was the fact that they all had insurance. Who provided the policy? Jesus! Who paid the premium? Jesus! Jesus, who is the king of kings and lord of lords, covered them. Jesus has the authority, control, and power to cover us. He is our master and chief who rules with holy power. We must recognize in Jesus, one with authority and power. His office is open twenty-four hours a day, seven days a week.

> *"Let us therefore come boldly unto the throne of grace, that we may obtain mercy, and find grace to help in time of need."* **Hebrews 4:16.**

Jesus is both willing and able to provide the coverage we need at no costs to us.

Why do we need this type of insurance? **Matthew 8:23-27** tells us that storms will come in our lives and we will need insurance. As the winds of unpaid bills blow, we will need insurance. As the thunder of little to no food claps, we will need insurance. As the lightning of unemployment strikes, we will need insurance. When the physicians have given us the worse news possible, we will need insurance. We will need to know that Jesus has us covered and has paid the price with His stripes. Whatever your circumstance is today, if you need to see the doctor, you are covered. If you need to pay utility bills, you are covered. If you need your sins forgiven, you are covered. You have the best insurance available to man; He is Jesus Christ, The Lord!

REFLECTIONS ON MATTHEW 9

LET GOD BE GOD

As **Matthew 9** begins, Jesus once again is healing but this first healing in our text is different in nature. While the disease (palsy) is the same, Jesus does something we have not witnessed in the book of Matthew up to this point.

> *"²And, behold, **they brought to him a man sick of the palsy, lying on a bed:** and **Jesus** seeing their faith **said unto the sick of the palsy; Son, be of good cheer; thy sins be forgiven thee."***

He does not address the physical sickness of this man but rather He addresses His spiritual sickness and tells him to cheer up because his sins have been forgiven. The only one who has this authority over sickness and sin is Jesus. In our daily experiences in life, we must let God be God. He knows exactly what He is doing on the behalf of man.

God declares his own sovereignty,

"¹⁴What shall we say then? Is there unrighteousness with God? God forbid. ¹⁵For he saith to Moses, I will have mercy on whom I will have mercy, and I will have compassion on whom I will have compassion. ¹⁶So then it is not of him that willeth, nor of him that runneth, but of God that sheweth mercy." Romans 9:14-16.

God has supreme power and is free any external control. God is unbounded. He cannot be held by any chemical or physical restraints. He is unlimited in His ability and has boundless intellect. God can do anything He wants to do, let God be God. Throughout history, there have been men and women who have claimed to have the power of the true and living God. However, a closer inquiry into their lives paint a different picture.

"Yes, just as you can identify a tree by its fruit, so you can identify people by their actions." Matthew 7:20 New Living Translation

God is not only a sovereign God but He is also a holy God. In **Matthew 9** Jesus is also accused of being immoral for socializing with sinners. Are we not all sinners,

"For everyone has sinned; we all fall short of God's glorious standard." Romans 3:23 New Living Translation

The fact that we are sinners indicates that we are in need of a savior. Only a person has the power and authority to save us, and that is Jesus. There is nothing we can do to save ourselves. Dressing in our finest clothing will not save us. Using the most eloquent of words will not save us. Eating a gluten free diet will not save us. Fasting for days or weeks at a time will not save us. We do not need any outward signs to prove how religious we are.

"Neither is there salvation in any other: for there is none other name under heaven given among men, whereby we must be saved." Acts 4:12.

Let God be God in your lives today. This will allow Him to help, heal and restore you to the place where you truly need to be.

REFLECTIONS ON MATTHEW 10

CHURCH FOR THE UNCHURCHED

Matthew 10 introduces us to twelve men who have been called by Jesus to follow Him. They meet the definition of what it means to be unchurched. Unchurched people are Christians but not connected with their church physically or with regard to its goals and mission. Consider for a moment those individuals who attend church but do not participate on any committees. Consider those individuals who may give financially to their church but do not attend any service or meetings. Think about those in church who pray for everything and everybody without lifting a finger when the time comes to meet needs. These are unchurched. These are the ones Jesus is calling to follow Him. These are the ones who become His disciples.

A disciple is one who follows another with the hope that eventually they will become like the one they follow. A Christian disciple is a believer who follows Christ and then offers his own imitation of Christ as model for others to follow. This is what Christ envisions for us to be, His disciples. Christ led by example and demonstrated in His daily life what His disciples should do with regard to their interaction with others. Christ called the twelve to go out and proclaim the good news of the gospel.

> *"⁵...Go not into the way of the Gentiles, and into any city of the Samaritans enter ye not: ⁶But go rather to the lost sheep of the house of Israel. ⁷And as ye go, preach, saying, The kingdom of heaven is at hand. ⁸Heal the sick, cleanse the lepers, raise the dead, cast out devils: freely ye have received, freely give." Matthew 10:7, 8.*

Do we understand what is happening here? Jesus is saying to his gospel messengers to go where the gospel is needed the most. He is encouraging them to go to those who are unchurched. It is not by chance that the disciples are called to go to those who are profess followers of Christ, church people. If those individuals who are professing a connection to Christ, church people, are hypocritical, there is no way they can reach anyone who may not know Him in any capacity.

Jesus gives them multiple examples of what they will face as they go out and proclaim the gospel.

"Behold, I send you forth as sheep in the midst of wolves: be ye therefore wise as serpents, and harmless as doves." **Matthew 10:16.**

The text implies that when we go out to proclaim the gospel of Jesus Christ, we will experience difficult and challenging people and situations. Whatever difficulty we face, we will never be alone. Often as followers of Christ we are faced with situations that may cause us to fear and not want to do the things that we are called to do. We must always remember that God is with us and if we are truly working for Him He will not leave us in any situation powerless.

When we realize we are representing the God of this universe, the same God who created this world, the same God who has never lost a battle, we will become brave and bold. As we go out as His messengers to share the gospel, with any who will give an ear to that word this promise is given.

"Fear thou not; for I am with thee: be not dismayed; for I am thy God: I will strengthen thee; yea, I will help thee; yea, I will uphold thee with the right hand of my righteousness." **Isaiah 41:10.**

REFLECTIONS ON MATTHEW 11

BELIEVING WITHOUT MIRACLES

"11 Verily I say unto you, Among them that are born of women there hath not risen a greater than John the Baptist: notwithstanding he that is least in the kingdom of heaven is greater than he."

Jesus solidifies the ministry of John the Baptist. At this time, John is in prison and he inquires of his disciples to see if Jesus is indeed the Messiah they have been looking for or is there someone else. The response of Christ is not what one might expect. Instead of Jesus going to the prison to visit John and tell him in person Jesus tells them to tell John what they have witnessed and heard. This should be enough for John to know who Jesus was. What had they seen and heard? They had seen the blind receive sight, the cripple walk, the diseases healed, the deaf able to hear and the dead raised.

What had they heard? They heard gospel preached to all men without prejudice or compromise.

Does God need to provide miraculous proof for us to believe that He is who He says He is? Absolutely not! In John's case, we see basic human nature. He just wants to know for himself. I am confident that when his disciples returned and gave him the report he was sure as to whom Jesus was because no man except the Son of the true and living God could do the things his disciples described to him. When we are imprisoned with debt, depression, loneliness and heartache, do we seek out Jesus? Do we want the assurance to know that He is truly the one who can help us in our time of need?

> *"¹²Then shall ye call upon me, and ye shall go and pray unto me, and I will hearken unto you. ¹³And ye shall seek me, and find me, when ye shall search for me with all your heart."*
> *Jeremiah 29:12, 13*

Regardless of our circumstances, however extreme they may be; does God need to provide miraculous evidence to demonstrate that He is who He is? Absolutely not! We must always remember that not every problem or difficult situation we find ourselves in requires a miracle. For example, if your vehicle has no gas in it and you need to go to work, this is not a miracle working moment. This is a go to the gas station moment. How can we be assured to know that God is who He declares that He is? We can look at our experiences with Him and notice a pattern. God has always met our needs without fail. Have you ever said, I remember when I needed something and God provided. I remember when I needed to pay something and God provided.

> *"Now glory be to God, who by his mighty power at work within us is able to do far more than we would ever dare to ask or even dream of—infinitely beyond our highest prayers, desires, thoughts, or hopes." Ephesians 3:20, The Living Bible.*

We must believe God without miracles.

Some people express a desire for a miracle because they want confirmation of the truth of God. Some people may look for a miracle because they do not believe what has previously been miraculously done by God. However, there comes a time when enough miracles have been performed. The truth is proven and clear. There comes a time when we have to exercise our faith.

"For we live by believing and not by seeing." 2 Corinthians 5:7 New Living Translation

While it may be challenging to trust God in our most difficult times, we must trust Him nonetheless.

"And those whose faith has made them good in God's sight must live by faith, trusting him in everything. Otherwise, if they shrink back, God will have no pleasure in them." Hebrews 10:38 The Living Bible.

Matthew 11 leaves us with an invitation and comforting words. We are invited to go to Jesus with any and everything that may burden us. We may be pressed down in every phase of our lives, physically, mentally, emotionally, financially, socially and spiritually. Reflect on what Christ has done for you in the past. It should give you great comfort and peace to know that this same Jesus will continue to help us in our time of extreme stress and pressure; whatever it is.

"28Come unto me, all ye that labour and are heavy laden, and I will give you rest. 29Take my yoke upon you, and learn of me; for I am meek and lowly in heart: and ye shall find rest unto your souls. 30For my yoke is easy, and my burden is light."
We can believe without miracles.

REFLECTIONS ON MATTHEW 12

WHO WANTS TO WORK ON THE SABBATH? I DO!

"8For the Son of man is Lord even of the sabbath day.:"

How did we get here? *Matthew 12* begins with Jesus and His disciples walking on the Sabbath day through the corn. The disciples were hungry and plucked the corn to eat it. Of course the Pharisees saw this and stated that the Disciples of Christ had broken the Sabbath by plucking the corn and eating it. There is a laundry lists of things that one supposedly cannot do on the Sabbath. Why focus on what we reportedly cannot do and find the things we can do. While we do not have to look for things to get in to on the Sabbath, we should not shy away from doing acceptable and wonderful acts on the Sabbath. "

> *And let us not be weary in well doing: for in due season we shall reap, if we faint not." Galatians 6:9*

Jesus Himself does a beautiful deed on the Sabbath by healing the man with the withered hand.

> *"Then saith he to the man, Stretch forth thine hand. And he stretched it forth; and it was restored whole, like as the other." Matthew 12:13.*

While there are biblical examples of doing good on the Sabbath, common sense has to factor in to some of the things we may encounter. Hospitals with religious connections operate on Sabbath. What would be the plight of people who were in these facilities if they had to wait to receive care from sunset every Friday until sunset on Saturday? This would be medical chaos and potentially dangerous for some.

While in the ministry, I had the opportunity to volunteer as a law enforcement chaplain for 20 years before retiring from that position in 2018 in Wichita Falls, Texas. Years ago I received a call from the dispatch center to go to the local hospital (around 5:00 am on a Saturday – the Sabbath) there had been a fire with one person severely injured. I was not given any information on who the injured individual was. Without hesitation, I got dressed and raced to the hospital. When I arrived, the person that injured was a close friend of my family. I was very pleased that I did not hesitate or make it a Sabbath keeping or Sabbath breaking moment. I prayed for my friend and prayed with the family before she was air lifted to the burn center in Dallas. While bearing the scars of the burns today, my friend is alive and thriving by the grace of God.

One of the most fulfilling things in this life is when we find our true purpose for living. When we think about doing the will of God, it is not a complicated feat. We should simply live as Christ-like as we can with regard to what we do and say. Do not attempt to rationalize it or complicate it. Keep it simple and do as Christ did. Treat others the way Jesus treated people and follow His word.

"Commit thy works unto the Lord, and thy thoughts shall be established." Proverbs 16:3.

REFLECTIONS ON MATTHEW 13

YOU REAP WHAT YOU SOW

"Be not deceived; God is not mocked: for whatsoever a man soweth, that shall he also reap." Galatians 6:7.

Do you consider yourself a sower? What exactly is a sower? A sower is someone who plants seeds for the production of a crop. He is a cultivator of land. This describes the physical aspects of a sower. Spiritually speaking we are sowers of the word of God. As we spread the seeds of the gospel, we must do our part and trust God for the results. There are many obstacles that we face when sharing the life giving word of God. We may encounter individuals who may reject the word of God. We may encounter some individuals who may accept the word of God. Then there are those who may accept the word of God for a moment and fall back. Do not despair; continue to sow, because we reap what we sow.

"So then neither is he that planteth anything, neither he that watereth; but God that giveth the increase." 1 Corinthians 3:7.

When the seeds of the word of God are planted, the result will not a church full of "righteous" members. We are not in a position to determine who is worthy of the pew or Christ. In due time the harvest will come.

"Let both grow together until the harvest: and in the time of harvest I will say to the reapers, Gather ye together first the tares, and bind them in bundles to burn them: but gather the wheat into my barn." Matthew 13:30.

How does the kingdom of heaven grow? How do families grow? How do communities grow? How do churches grow? They grow one person at a time just like the planting of the seed.

We should never become discouraged because the church is not full or people are not responding in the way we think they should to the gospel. God's kingdom in the end will be full. When we decide to want to be a part of the kingdom of heaven, our lives must be transformed.

"Don't copy the behavior and customs of this world, but let God transform you into a new person by changing the way you think. Then you will learn to know God's will for you, which is good and pleasing and perfect." Romans 12:1 New Living Bible.

The transformation of a person takes place from the inside out. It is not the clothes we wear or the vehicle we drive that demonstrates a true Christ like transformation in our lives. It is the changing of the heart and mind that true conversion of the person takes place.

It is imperative for us to know that we truly need Christ through this transformation process. We must be willing to make any sacrifice to become the person that Christ intends for us to be. The kingdom of heaven is available to all men, women, boys and girls. There is no prejudice or hatred related to the kingdom of God. There are no social or physical divides in the kingdom of God. There are no ethnic or cultural divides in the kingdom of God. There is no discrimination I the kingdom of God. Even though the kingdom of heaven is available to all, not everyone will make a choice to be a part of His kingdom. To be a sower requires dedication, perseverance, patience and total dependency on Jesus for a super-abundant result.

"Remember this—a farmer who plants only a few seeds will get a small crop. But the one who plants generously will get a generous crop." 2 Corinthians 9:6 New Living Translation.

REFLECTIONS ON MATTHEW 14

KEEP YOUR HEAD ON IN THE STORM

"³For Herod had laid hold on John, and bound him, and put him in prison for Herodias' sake, his brother Philip's wife... ¹⁰And he sent, and beheaded John in the prison."

This is what happens when a person cannot control his/her passions on any level. We have King Herod who is in a relationship (committing adultery) with his brother's wife. He is called out by the preaching of John the Baptist. There is no remorse or repentance; instead, he puts John in jail. He then ultimately cuts off his head. Self-control is something we all struggle with at some point or another in life. This is a classic example of how we can spiral down and never be able to recover. The king was an adulterer who became a murderer all because he had no control of himself. We often say, what we would not do or where we would never go, yet without self-control we will find ourselves doing some unimaginable things. We must learn to keep our wits in the midst of trying times.

> *"¹⁵And when it was evening, his disciples came to him, saying, This is a desert place, and the time is now past; send the multitude away, that they may go into the villages, and buy themselves victuals... ²¹And they that had eaten were about five thousand men, beside women and children.."* Matthew 14:15 & 21.

If there ever was a time for someone to lose his or her head in a storm, this was the time. Can you imagine what it would truly cost to feed this amount of people, even in the time of Jesus? There was no panic or stress on the part of Jesus. He takes five loaves and two fish and does what would seem to be an impossible task. This is not the first time Jesus miraculously provided food. *1 Kings 17* tells us how Elijah was fed by ravens. Jesus is not in the business of watching His creation go hungry physically or spiritually under any circumstance. The storm of hunger is real. Hold this promise close to your heart.

> *"...bread shall be given him; his waters shall be sure."* Isaiah 33:16.

Keep your head on in the storm.

> *"But the ship was now in the midst of the sea, tossed with waves: for the wind was contrary."* Matthew 14:24.

Have you ever been in a storm on the sea? In 1994, my wife and I took a cruise on the Atlantic Ocean. Returning back to port there was a storm in the ocean and that huge cruise ship swayed back and forth like a piece of paper in the wind. All I could say was Lord please do not let me die like this. Jesus is always present, even in the midst of enormous storms that hit out lives. We have to be able to recognize Jesus. We must know and recognize His voice. It is easy for us to distinguish Jesus when the sun is shining and the wind is calm. It is easy to recognize Jesus when the bills are paid and the pantry is full. However, when days are dark and nights are long the assurance is that Jesus is always present with us.

"God is our refuge and strength, a very present help in trouble."
Psalm 46:1.

Keep your head on in the storm.

How many of us have said Lord if you are God then send the money for my bills? Lord if you are God then send me my soulmate. Lord if you are God then give me this new car. There is no "if" He is God, He is! We need to recognize who we are in His presence even in the midst of a storm. When we begin to sink in our storm (just like Peter), Jesus immediately comes to our aid and provides exactly what we need. He is the same God in times of peace as well as times of difficulty. Call on Him in the storm and Jesus will renew our faith in Him.

"Behold, the Lord's hand is not shortened, that it cannot save; neither his ear heavy, that it cannot hear:" Isaiah 59:1.

Keep your head on in the storm.

REFLECTIONS ON MATTHEW CHAPTER 15
"TRADITION VERSES THE BIBLE"

"⁹But in vain they do worship me, teaching for doctrines the commandments of men."

Tradition can be summed up as an inherited, established, or customary pattern of thought, action, or behavior such as a religious practice or a social custom. The Jews had a great deal of traditions and rules related to eating including what to eat and how to eat. In addition, they had rules governing the wearing of garments. There are too many to mention, which would require a volume of books on its own. Teaching the traditions of men when they go contrary to God's word can be very problematic. Man can make many rules especially in the church settings. We have enough biblical instruction on how to live without man creating his own set of personal rules to make sure that someone is trodden under foot.

While places of worship need guidelines and structure, they should not have nonbiblical guidelines. Think about that for a second and consider some of the rules and guidelines you may find in your personal church manuals. Are these rules and guidelines based in bible principles? Are they written in such a manner that Christ is glorified? Traditions can be harsh and regimented. Love has to be the foundation on which our teachings, rules and guidelines are based.

> *"Finally, be you all of one mind, having compassion one of another, love as brothers, be pitiful, be courteous:"* 1 Peter 3:8.

Have you ever heard this phrase at work or church, this is how we have always done things. While traditions might be nice in a family setting, they can be disastrous in the Christian world. If you think about it long enough, tradition can cause us to become complacent and predictable. When you reflect on your worship experience or even how your church conducts its business, do you see the traditions of men over riding the word of God? When we hold to our traditions, it can prevent us from thriving in Christ.

> *"The righteous keep moving forward, and those with clean hands become stronger and stronger." Job 17:9. New Living Translation.*

Love should be the motivating factor in all that we do and say. Some traditions can prevent professed people of God from doing all that they can for their fellowman. How would your local church respond to a nonmember asking for financial assistance if your church had a tradition (History) of only assisting church members? The example we should follow is not that of man but of Jesus Christ.

> *"And, behold, a woman of Canaan came out of the same coasts, and cried unto him, saying, Have mercy on me, O Lord, thou son of David; my daughter is grievously vexed with a devil." Matthew 15:22.*

She was not a "church" member or one of them. That did not prevent Jesus from helping this grieving mother.

"Then Jesus answered and said unto her, O woman, great is thy faith: be it unto thee even as thou wilt. And her daughter was made whole from that very hour." Matthew 15:28.

She was not a member of His religious sect. She was not an upstanding pillar of the community. She was just a woman who had a devil-possessed child that needed help. Do not allow any nonbiblical teaching to guide you in your dealings with anyone. The Bible is our sure guide. Are you willing to follow it today?

REFLECTIONS ON MATTHEW 16

JESUS, THE ROCK STAR

"¹³When Jesus came into the coasts of Caesarea Philippi, he asked his disciples, saying, Whom do men say that I the Son of man am? ¹⁴And they said, Some say that thou art John the Baptist: some, Elias; and others, Jeremias, or one of the prophets. ¹⁵He saith unto them, But whom say ye that I am? ¹⁶And Simon Peter answered and said, Thou art the Christ, the Son of the living God."

Looking at the responses it was obvious that many men did not know who Jesus truly was. Then Jesus asked the question of those who were the closest to Him who they thought He was. Now it gets interesting. Everyone hand should have been raised. Only Peter replied with the answer. He separates Jesus from the false, pagan gods. He acknowledges that Jesus is the one and only Christ, the Anointed One, the Messiah. The Son of the true and living God. Words like anointed and even messiah are thrown around a lot in religious circles. We have seen false messiahs in our society and there is not a day that goes by that some pastor, prophet, or religious teacher claim "the anointing". When men recognize who Jesus truly is they would shrink back from loosely using these terms to reference themselves with. There is but one Christ, the Anointed One, the Messiah and His name is Jesus.

"¹⁸And I say also unto thee, That thou art Peter, and upon this rock I will build my church; and the gates of hell shall not prevail against it."

Many people think that since Peter has the correct answer that he is rewarded with being the foundation of the church. It has been said and taught in some places that Peter was the first pope. I am not sure how these teachings get started but nothing could be further from the truth. Jesus acknowledges who Peter is and then states that the church will be established upon *"…this rock…"* The question that has caused great confusion among many religions is whether the church is established on Peter and is Peter *"…this rock…"* that is referenced in the text. You must realize is that God's church is not and could not be established on any man. Now I will attempt to give us a brief lesson in Greek that should clear up any confusion on who Peter is and who *"…this rock…"* that the church is established on is.

Peter "petros" Petros: a rock, a detached stone that might be thrown or easily moved. Peter can be recognized as a rock, he is not the rock on which the church is founded. **"this rock…" "petra" Petra: a mass of rock, unmovable force. Christ can only be referring to Himself. He is the only firm foundation. Remember the wise man that built his house upon "the rock".** He did not build his house upon a petros Petros – a detached stone that could be easily moved. **He built his house on a petra Petra – a mass of rock, an unmovable force, a sure and firm foundation, (Same word used in both text PETRA) the church is founded and established on Jesus Christ.** There is a clear distinction from PETRA concerning the Lord Himself, the sure foundation, the unmovable mass of rock and PETROS concerning Peter the apostle who could be easily moved about.

> *"Christ is also the head of the church, which is his body…"*
> *Colossians 1:18, New Living Translation.*

The pastor is not the head of the church. The elder is not the head of the church. The deacon is not the head of the church. The parishioner who gives the most money is not the head of the church. The most prominent family is not the head of the church. There is only room for one Rock Star and His name is Jesus.

REFLECTIONS ON MATTHEW 17

FAITH AND BELIEF DOES NOT RUB OFF

"¹⁵Lord, have mercy on my son: for he is lunatick, and sore vexed: for ofttimes he falleth into the fire, and oft into the water."

Imagine having a parent say to you my son is a lunatic, he is jumping in fire and then in water please help me. Just because the disciples were hanging around Jesus did not mean that the power of Christ was just going to rub off on them. They were unable to help this man. No one can possess another man's faith and belief. Some individuals think that as long as someone is praying for them they can do whatever they want to do because they are covered. We all must have a personal relationship with Christ; this is not a group effort. Our personal experiences will dictate how firm our personal faith in Christ is.

What is faith? Faith is having firm persuasion or belief. Faith is having a conviction based purely on hearing, not seeing, touching, smelling or tasting.

"Now faith is assurance of things hoped for, a conviction of things not seen." Hebrews 11:1, American Standard Version.

The bible does not say that faith comes by seeing and touching. It does not say that faith comes by smelling and tasting. The word of God says,

"So then faith cometh by hearing, and hearing by the word of God." Romans 10:17.

Each of us hears God's word as it speaks to us personally and therefore our relationship with God is personal. We have to believe God's word and apply it appropriately in every situation we find ourselves in. Faith is not transferable and it does not rub off.

Unbelief can cause fear to take hold of our lives and emotions. Faith and fear cannot coexist. Faith is the opposite of unbelief. There should be no fear when we are faced with situations that we cannot see our way through. Fear is a human reaction to the trials and difficulties that we will face in this life, but God will give us just what we need to deal with the trials and difficulties. Without trials, our faith does not increase. God knows our weaknesses and fears, but He provides comfort in His word through these words.

"And the peace of God, which passeth all understanding, shall keep your hearts and minds through Christ Jesus." Philippians 4:7.

Faith allows us to obey God and follow Him even while going through our most challenging trials. We are God's people and must follow His plain word,

"For therein is the righteousness of God revealed from faith to faith: as it is written, The just shall live by faith." Romans 1:17.

REFLECTIONS ON MATTHEW 18

DO YOU OWE ANYONE MONEY?

"²³Therefore is the kingdom of heaven likened unto a certain king, which would take account of his servants. ²⁴And when he had begun to reckon, one was brought unto him, which owed him ten thousand talents." Matthew 18:23, 24.

We all have borrowed money from either a family member or a bank. Some may say I have never borrowed any money from anyone or any source. If you have ever financed a car or even purchased a house with a mortgage, you have borrowed money. If you have used a credit card and have a balance, you have essentially borrowed money. If there came a time where you could not pay back what you have borrowed or used what has been the outcome? We call the person and ask for time to repay them, as we would do with the mortgage lender or Credit Card Company. If our request is granted, we are extremely happy with those results. But what happens when we see someone who owes us two dollars. We act as if they owe us a millions dollars. Every time we see the person who owes us the two dollars we have the same speech, you have my two dollars.

God has forgiven us for some horrible, disgusting, unthinkable things and yet at times we struggle to forgive our wives, husbands, brothers, sisters, neighbors, co-workers and even a stranger we may encounter.

"²¹Then came Peter to him, and said, Lord, how oft shall my brother sin against me, and I forgive him? till seven times? ²²Jesus saith unto him, I say not unto thee, Until seven times: but, Until seventy times seven." Matthew 18:21, 22.

We cannot put a count on how many times to forgive someone that has wronged us in some way. It is a good practice as a professed Christian to forgive anyone for anything they have done to us at any time. It will also serve us well to forgive others we may feel owes us anything. As we remember what God has done for us on a moment by moment basis with regard to our issues; it will become a part of our character to do the same for others. God has taken a personal interest in us and will do anything He can to reconcile us back to Himself. He goes after us when we are lost. He forgives us when we falter and fail. Everyone deserves to be treated with compassion especially those who have asked for our forgiveness, patience and mercy.

"⁷Give to everyone what you owe them: Pay your taxes and government fees to those who collect them, and give respect and honor to those who are in authority. ⁸Owe nothing to anyone—except for your obligation to love one another. If you love your neighbor, you will fulfill the requirements of God's law." Romans 13:7, 8, New Living Translation.

Ask yourself, do you anyone money?

REFLECTIONS ON MATTHEW 19

CAN TWO BECOME ONE? GOD'S MATHEMATICS

"³The Pharisees also came unto him, tempting him, and saying unto him, Is it lawful for a man to put away his wife for every cause?"

The institution of marriage today is being tested on many fronts. In our text the question is brought to Jesus concerning the putting away of a man's wife for every cause. During the time of Moses men were allowed to put their wives away for just about any reason. Some couples today would jump at that because we live in a society where if things do not go our way or we do not find ourselves as satisfied with the condition of our relationship, we want to change partners and move on quickly.

There is one word used in the text where two can become one in a marriage relationship and that word is, "Cleave" - **"kallw" kallo** – The Greek word used here means to join fast together, to glue, to cement.

We have to come to understand that no matter what we are facing in our relationships, we must remain glued and cemented to each other. God has always accomplished miraculous results with numbers. Remember the two separate feedings of the multitudes. On one occasion, there were 5,000 fed with five loaves and two fish and on the other occasion, 4,000 were fed with seven loaves and a few fish. The numbers do not make sense, but the results are amazing. It is mind blowing to comprehend how two people can become one. That is exactly what happens when you are cemented to one another in Christ.

We may not understand the concept of this equation but we must accept the results.

> *"Therefore shall a man leave his father and his mother, and shall cleave unto his wife: and they shall be one flesh."*
> *Genesis 2:24.*

The beauty of what Christ does is that while we become one, we still maintain our individuality. Now that is a miracle. Do not be too quick to change spouses just because of old age, sickness, finances or a change in social status. Do not be too quick to change spouses for any reason, give God the opportunity to do what He does best and that is work on our behalf. While two can become one in the marriage relationship, we also can become one with Christ. *Matthew 19* gives us insight as to how we can become one with Christ. Jesus said,

> *"If you want to be complete, go, sell what you own, and give the money to the poor. Then you will have treasure in heaven. And come follow me." Matthew 19:21, Common English Bible.*

There is no better way to get to the kingdom of God than by being glued to Him. The closer we get to Him the more we become reflectors of His character. Can two become one? According to the word of God, yes. Would you like to become one with Christ today?

REFLECTIONS ON MATTHEW 20
"IT'S PAYDAY"

"¹⁰But when the first came, they supposed that they should have received more; and they likewise received every man a penny."

Can you remember what payday was like thirty or forty years ago? Most paydays were on Friday. You would receive your check, head to the bank to either cash your check or deposit it into your account. Over the years you move from paper checks to direct deposit, and now payday is even more exciting because you know at midnight prior to the true payday your money is in your banking institution. As your place of employment grows more workers are hired. You have been there for many years and may be getting close to retirement. As paydays come and go you discover that some of the newly hired workers are receiving the same amount of income as you. What would you do in a situation like this? In Matthew 20 those who had been on the job longer they had deserved more money since they had worked longer. They had forgotten one small detail.

"For the kingdom of heaven is like unto a man that is an householder, which went out early in the morning to hire labourers into his vineyard. ²And when he had agreed with the labourers for a penny a day, he sent them into his vineyard." Matthew 20:1, 2.

They were hired first and had agreed on a price for the work they were to perform.

Who does not like to be first? Being first does not necessarily mean you receive the most or are entitled to anything. For example: being first to the dinner table does not mean you get more on your plate than anyone else does. Everyone at the table should get their share of food that has been prepared.

"So the last shall be first, and the first last: for many be called, but few chosen." Matthew 20:16.

Some have the mistaken belief that if they are born into the right religion or family they are entitled to more and should be first. Some believe those who are first through the church doors or give the most tithes and offerings will be favored in heaven. Those who were not first through the church doors or gave high amounts financially will receive an equal reward with those who have been faithful the longest. The ultimate payday is coming very soon.

"The wages of the righteous is life, but the earnings of the wicked are sin and death." Proverbs 10:16, New International Version.

REFLECTIONS ON MATTHEW 21

WE SHOULD KNOW BY NOW

"¹⁰And when he was come into Jerusalem, all the city was moved, saying, Who is this? ¹¹And the multitude said, This is Jesus the prophet of Nazareth of Galilee."

One would think that after all that He had done in every place that He had been all men would know who Jesus was. How is it that today people have the same question as to who Jesus is? He reveals Himself through His word both spoken and read. He reveals Himself to us in hymns. He reveals Himself through meditation and prayer. We must come to know His voice and His way of revealing Himself to us and then we would have no question as to who He is. Many have claimed to be Christ through the years but if we examine closely these individuals, we will discover that nothing about them at any point and time revealed that they were Christ. Many men, women, boys and girls are truly seeking Jesus. With many claiming to prophets, pastors, healers and spiritual teachers, it is easy to see how one could be confused.

Jesus was constantly questioned about His God given authority. He often found Himself defending something He had done, miraculous or otherwise. Jesus never engages in a verbal confrontation with anyone. He simply uses His own words in parables and direct bible quotes and allows the hearers to almost answer their own questions. One or two things will happen when either this occurs, the individual will conclude or they will go away with more questions. When we read the word of God for ourselves and share that word with others, we should leave no doubt, as to whom

Jesus is. The best witness is telling people exactly what Christ has done and is doing for us. No one can argue with a living example of what Christ has done and is doing on his or her behalf.

We should know by now who Jesus is. All we have to do is remember the good things He has done for us. Take time right now and make a list of the good things Jesus has done for you. He has given us another day of life. He has sustained us through times of peace and times of strife. He has protected us from seen and unseen dangers. He has provided for us both physical and spiritual food. He comforts us in our most sorrowful times. He rejoices with us in our happy moments. He provides for our material needs, some of which we do not deserve. He loves us with unconditional love. This obviously is a short list.

"What can I give back to the Lord for all the good things he has done for me?" Psalm 116:12, Common English Bible.

Praise Him today for who He is. Worship Him today for who He is. Glorify Him today for who He is. Love Him today for who He is.

REFLECTIONS ON MATTHEW 22

CAKE AND ICE CREAM IN HEAVEN

"¹And Jesus answered and spake unto them again by parables, and said, ²The kingdom of heaven is like unto a certain king, which made a marriage for his son…"

Who doesn't appreciate being invited somewhere? We all like to be a part of joyful occasions especially when there is good food involved. When our oldest daughter turned three years old, we planned a birthday party for her at the pavilion at the local zoo. We reserved a special spot. We made plans to bring all the children we invited to the zoo after the party. My wife and I had planned to pay for every child and every parent; all they had to do was arrive at the pavilion. We had balloons, snacks and a cake. We were ready for the party but a strange thing happened. It began to rain slightly and no one came to the party. We were very disappointed when no one came to our baby's birthday party. My wife was doing her residency physician's training at the local Children's Hospital (It was located a few blocks from the zoo) and she had a great idea. She went to the hospital and asked if we could have our child's birthday party in one of the open areas of the hospital and invite some of the children who were able to attend from one of the floors of the hospital. The medical staff permitted it. It was the best birthday ever. All that was required from the children who could attend the party was their presence. Everything they could want in a party was provided for them. There was cake and ice cream for everyone. We even shared the gifts for our daughter with the children in the hospital.

Christ has prepared everything for us with regard not only to our present but also to our future. We are invited every day to have fellowship with Christ and that fellowship is on His terms. He prepares the place and the food for fellowship with us. Everything that is prepared for us will more than satisfy our need. Think about it, every day a feast of fellowship is provided for us. Accepting the invitation and going is all we have to do. When it comes to fellowship with Chirst, there should be no excuses. There will be work responsibilities and things to do around the house, but nothing is more important than spending time with God. Nothing in our lives should prevent us from this time of fellowship.

Think about the ultimate fellowship we will share in the kingdom of God. Everything is prepared for us all we have to do is accept the invitation. Housing, food, and clothes have been prepared for us. Every person will have ample opportunity to decide if they want to accept this invitation.

"But as it is written, Eye hath not seen, nor ear heard, neither have entered into the heart of man, the things which God hath prepared for them that love him." 2 Corinthians 2:9.

REFLECTIONS ON MATTHEW 23

TAKE OFF YOUR MASKS

"Woe unto you scribes and Pharisees, hypocrites..." Matthew 23:14.

One of the greatest challenges we have in church is keeping our youth involved and engaged in the total religious experience. Not just what takes place during the church service but even with those activities outside of the church. When religion is seen as a burden or something that is difficult to navigate, both the youth and the adults will struggle to find their place. Often when the minister stands in the pulpit to preach the word of God, the minister does the speaking and the people do the listening. Preaching a convicting word is totally different than telling people how bad they are and what they need to do to get themselves together. No one attends church to be constantly reminded that they are sinners. The problem has been identified, now it is time for the good news of the gospel to be presented to us. The gospel has to be presented in love.

When anyone is made to feel like they have to keep a ton of rules and follow too many guidelines the easy solution is to just walk away. Many rules seem to just fit the whims of those in charge. Great caution must be taken when following the guidelines of men that are deficit of biblical teachings. It becomes easy to tell other people what to do while in the pulpit or leading the meetings, but no one should be subjected to anything that goes against biblical principles. We should aspire to be builders of the kingdom of God. The kingdom of God cannot be built with rules and guidelines. People are not drawn to Christ following "the rules" that man has put in place.

In many churches and religious organizations, the pastors and leaders are placed on high pedestals. In some cases, they are revered. So revered that when they speak regardless of what they may be saying the people are taking it for the truth. Not all religious leaders are truly working for God and the building of His kingdom. There is a saying, many are called, few are chosen, and some just got up and went! You have to be able to tell the sheep from the wolves.

"Watch out for false teachers. They come to you dressed as if they were sheep. On the inside they are hungry wolves." Matthew 7:15, New Life Version.

The masks must come off.

THE ART OF ILLUSION

"⁴And Jesus answered and said unto them, Take heed that no man deceive you. ⁵For many shall come in my name, saying, I am Christ; and shall deceive many."

Let's define the word deceive. It means to cause someone to believe something that is not true, typically in order to gain some personal advantage, or to give a mistaken impression.

No one likes to be tricked or deceived. We would like to think that the people we deal with will be honest and truthful, especially those who profess to work for Christ. The warning is given over and over in God's word to be extremely careful when listening to and following after those who are supposed to be building up the kingdom of God. We have seen in the past many individuals claiming to be Jesus Christ or The Messiah; only for us to find out that they were absolutely false. They all seem to preach a message of hope and some type of social and financial prosperity. They all appear to be loving and accepting of everyone. However, when the dust settles and the curtain is pulled back they are proven to be deceivers. How many lives have been lost physically to these so called leaders and prophets of Christ? How many families have been torn apart as a result of someone leading individuals down the wrong religious path? A bigger question, how many souls have been lost for all eternity for following after one of these self-proclaimed religious leaders?

"²³Then if any man shall say unto you, Lo, here is Christ, or there; believe it not. ²⁴For there shall arise false Christs, and false prophets, and shall shew great signs and wonders; insomuch that, if it were possible, they shall deceive the very elect. ²⁵Behold, I have told you before. ²⁶Wherefore if they shall say unto you, Behold, he is in the desert; go not forth: behold, he is in the secret chambers; believe it not."

While it is easy to associate some false prophets with tele-evangelist and faith healers, have you ever given thought to those false prophets who may be in your local churches? If you think long and hard enough you may come up with that special someone who always had the answers to every bible question. They always seem to be closer to Christ than everyone else. They appear to have all the gifts needed for ministry and have no qualms about demonstrating them in any setting they find themselves. This is just something for you to think about. Anyone claiming to be Christ or The Messiah here on earth is not to be believed by any professed Christian under any circumstance. We can never allow our emotions or problems lead us to a false hope found in a false spiritual leader.

The bible has always been plain and clear as to who Jesus is and how He will return.

> *"For the Lord himself will descend from heaven with a cry of command, with the voice of an archangel, and with the sound of the trumpet of God. And the dead in Christ will rise first. Then we who are alive, who are left, will be caught up together with them in the clouds to meet the Lord in the air, and so we will always be with the Lord." 1 Thessalonians 4:16-17.*

There is no ambiguity. God has always separated Himself from the false gods and false prophets. From the very beginning God has separated Himself by doing the one thing that only the true and living God can do, create.

> *"In the beginning God created the heaven and the earth." Genesis 1:1.*

False gods and false prophets may come up with a trick or two, but only the true and living God has the distinction of creating something from nothing.

There is one major sign that we can look for when detecting a false Christ. When there is an emphasis on the day and the time of the appearing of this alleged Christ; we should not entertain this teaching under any circumstance. "

> *But of that day and hour knoweth no man, no, not the angels of heaven, but my Father only." Matthew 24:36.*

We can trust His word, it plainly tells us that He will return. Are you ready for Jesus to come?

REFLECTIONS ON MATTHEW 25

WHAT IS YOUR DEFENSE?

"Watch therefore, for ye know neither the day nor the hour wherein the Son of man cometh." Matthew 25:13.

There is no viable reason that we can give for being unprepared for the coming of Jesus. While we can make any excuse we like, there is none that will be acceptable. There is no argument that we can make as to why we are unprepared. The freedom of choice we have as individuals and Christians is something that we should never take for granted. The choices we make in life have consequences. Consequences that can lead to bountiful blessings or our ultimate downfall. Knowing Christ will come is one thing; being prepared for His coming is something totally different. We have heard the preaching of God's word for years proclaiming that Jesus is coming. How many of our loved ones have gone to their graves looking for the glorious appearing of Jesus Christ? Jesus is coming and yet He has not arrived yet! The fact that He has not come does not mean that He will not come.

"For yet a little while, and he that shall come will come, and will not tarry." Hebrews 10:3.

God has given us everything we need in order to be ready when He returns. It is up to us how we use these resources. What is your defense for not being ready?

There is no viable reason that we can give for being unfaithful as we wait for the return of Jesus. We live in a society of entitlement. Some people feel entitled to things that may not even belong to them. There are also some who feel entitled to the kingdom for various reasons. The body of Christ is made up of individuals from every walk of life. We also possess different gifts and talents. There are some who have multiple talents and gifts while others have minimal talents and gifts. Whatever gift or talent we have it is to be used for God's glory. No gift is wasted or too small in the building of God's kingdom. Do you recognize what gifts and talents God has given to you? What is the one gift or talent that God gives every-one that they can use on a daily basis? God gives us the gift of influence! Influence is the capacity to have an effect on the character, development, or behavior of someone or something. We all possess influence, how we use it will determine our personal spiritual growth. It can be used positively or negatively. Decide today how you will use your influence.

"Whatever work you do, do it with all your heart. Do it for the Lord and not for men." Colossians 3:23. New Life Version.

What is your defense for being faithful?

There is no viable reason that we can give for being unmotivated knowing that Christ will return. An unmotivated person has no interest in or enthusiasm for work or study. We all should know by now that we cannot work our way to the kingdom. We cannot get to the kingdom without doing some work with regard to our fellowman. There are some basic needs that we can meet for anyone, such as food, water and clothing. Regardless to what the people look like or smell like. Regardless to where they live or whether they are walking or driving.

Whether it be a stranger or someone we know, everyone deserves to be shown true heartfelt compassion. Even in the face of our own adversities we can find time to extend to someone else the love and compassion that Christ demonstrates towards us every day.

There will be individuals in the kingdom of God who may not have ever sang a hymn or understood all the prophecies in the bible. There will be individuals in God's kingdom who would not be able to differentiate between a church doctrine and a traditional belief. They will be in the kingdom because they were kind hearted towards those who were hurting.

"So let's not get tired of doing what is good. At just the right time we will reap a harvest of blessing if we don't give up." Galatians 6:9. New Living Translation.

What is your defense for not being unmotivated?

REFLECTIONS ON MATTHEW 26
PRESSURE WILL MAKE A PIPE BURST

"³³Peter answered and said unto him, Though all men shall be offended because of thee, yet will I never be offended. ³⁴Jesus said unto him, Verily I say unto thee, That this night, before the cock crow, thou shalt deny me thrice." Matthew 26:33, 34.

Pressure will make a pipe burst. What a statement. Often time's men say things that they truly believe in the heat of the moment. Men like to show their inner and outer strengths. Jesus had been explaining to His disciples for a while how He was going to be betrayed and crucified. These men proclaimed boldly that they would be willing to die for Christ. Have you ever made a commitment to the Lord wholeheartedly believing it; only to have to take it back once you are faced with pressure? Have you ever had a family member or friend turn their backs on you in at a time when you needed them the most? Would you turn you back on Jesus today for any reason? Nothing should be able to separate us from Jesus.

> *"What will separate us from the love Christ has for us? Can trouble, distress, persecution, hunger, nakedness, danger, or violent death separate us from his love?" Romans 8:35. God's Word Translation*

Jesus was sold out for thirty pieces of silver (**Matthew 26:15**). Some people sell Jesus for less than that on a daily basis. Some sell Him for a relationship. Some sell Him for fame and fortune. Some sell Him for simple recreation. Remember, pressure will make a pipe burst. Our actions very often determine who we truly are not our words. It is easy to say what we will or will not do given certain circumstances. Truth be told, we do not know what we will do when the pressure is placed upon us. When we are called to stand for Christ, do we boldly speak His word? When we are called to defend our faith, do we boldly speak the words that leaves no doubt as to who we are and what we believe? When we are called to stand on biblical principles in an undisciplined environment, do we stand on God's word even in the face of ridicule and backlash? Have you sold Jesus for anything that you can think of? Do not despair; we can always seek the forgiveness of Christ.

"If we confess our sins, he is faithful and just to forgive us our sins, and to cleanse us from all unrighteousness." 1 John 1:9.

While we may fail at times in our walk with Christ, all he requires is that we do our absolute best. In our weakest moments when the pressure is on us, we are covered by the grace of Christ.

"And he said unto me, My grace is sufficient for thee: for my strength is made perfect in weakness..." 2 Corinthians 12:9.

REFLECTIONS ON MATTHEW 27

JUSTICE DENIED

"²¹The governor answered and said unto them, Whether of the twain will ye that I release unto you? They said, Barabbas. ²²Pilate saith unto them, What shall I do then with Jesus which is called Christ? They all say unto him, Let him be crucified." Matthew 27:21, 22.

You would expect to go to court and get a fair and honest trial. You would expect that the judge as well as the jury handling your case would be unaffected by the people in the courtroom. You would expect the proceedings to be morally correct and fair. It is very difficult to keep your composure knowing that you are innocent of any wrongdoing while being convicted for an unexplainable offense. It is a basic human character trait to want justice in an obvious case of an accused person's innocence. The sentence for your unexplained offense is death. To make matters worse, while you get the death sentence a true criminal is set free. Justice in your case has been denied.

There was nothing fair about the trial, conviction and sentence given to Jesus. What had Jesus done for justice to be denied in His case?

Have you noticed during this mockery of justice that there were no witnesses called on behalf of Jesus? Have you noticed that Jesus did not have any representation? Have you noticed that Jesus never makes a statement in His own defense?

"And he answered him to never a word; insomuch that the governor marvelled greatly." Matthew 27:14.

Even while being mocked and ridiculed by both the soldiers and the crowd, there is no response from Jesus.

> *"Jesus, when he had cried again with a loud voice, yielded up the ghost." Matthew 27:50.*

Death may be many things. Death can be devastating, destructive, disgusting, and unwelcomed. For the Christian death is not a defeating foe. Jesus attempted on many occasions to tell his disciples that while He had to die, He would come back to them. We have that same assurance not only that Christ will come back for us but that those who die in the Lord will come back as well. Death does not worry about the age of those it takes out, infants, adolescents, teens, young adults, middle age, and elderly; everyone is vulnerable to this uncertain certainty. Death does not discriminate about one's religion, social status, financial status, or ethnicity.

> *"And as it is appointed unto men once to die, but after this the judgment:" Hebrews 9:27.*

REFLECTIONS ON MATTHEW 28

THE ORIGINAL ROLLING STONE

> *"⁶He is not here: for he is risen, as he said. Come, see the place where the Lord lay." Revelation 28:6.*

These are three of the most exciting words in the bible, *"...he is risen..."* The Greek word here **"egeirw"** (egeiro) "...to wake up, rise up, to be raised, with regard to people to be raised from the dead..." This has significance because the word means that Christ was risen beyond any doubt. There could be no question to this rising. We should have no doubt about the death of our loved ones or even our own death when the time comes because the promise here is clear, we will rise up as He has risen. If we have died with the faith and hope of one day seeing Christ in His kingdom, we will rise again.

> *"⁸Now if we be dead with Christ, we believe that we shall also live with him: ⁹Knowing that Christ being raised from the dead dieth no more; death hath no more dominion over him." Romans 6:8, 9.*

Christ did not go to the grave wondering if He would ever get up again. We can be confident even in the face of death that if we have followed Christ and have done our absolute best, we will rise again to enter into His eternal kingdom.

It is important for us to become acquainted with the voice of Christ. For it will be at His command that we are called from the grave.

> *"[16]For the Lord himself will come down from heaven with a commanding shout, with the voice of the archangel, and with the trumpet call of God. First, the believers who have died will rise from their graves." 1 Thessalonians 4:16. New Living Translation.*

We will respond to the voice of Christ from the grave because it is recognizable to us. It is a familiar voice. It is the same voice spoke to us in the midnight hours. It is the same voice comforted us in the loss of a loved one. It is that same voice that encouraged us when we needed it the most. It is that same voice that joined us in singing the hymns. It is that same voice that answered our prayers. When Jesus returns, we will respond to His voice as we always have. Let me give you an example.

Consider the work of a magnet. A magnet is a very special metal. When a magnet goes near a special kind of metal or other magnets, it will pull, or attract the other metal or magnet closer. It does not have to touch in order for the other metal or magnets to respond, it is automatically pulled toward the main magnet. It is the same when Christ comes again. He commands the dead in Christ to come forth from the grave. The dead in Christ hear His voice and respond as they always did and immediately go up to meet Him in the air. Headstones will be rolling that day.

> *"I am he that liveth, and was dead; and, behold, I am alive for evermore, Amen; and have the keys of hell and of death." Revelation 1:18.*

This is the blessed hope of Christian believers, that when Christ comes again, He will take us to be with Him for eternity. Are you ready for Jesus to come? Do you recognize His voice today?

"Scripture says, "If you hear God speak today, don't be stubborn. Don't be stubborn like those who rebelled." Hebrews 3:15. God's Word Translation.

As we wait for His return, reflect on these words.

"...and, lo, I am with you always, even unto the end of the world. Amen." Matthew 28:20.

REFLECTIONS ON
THE BOOK OF MARK

THE GOOD NEWS

This first chapter of the Gospel according to Mark is very intriguing. Mark is actually writing the story as Peter told him about Jesus. It begins with Jesus' ministry as he began. John the Baptist baptizing Jesus after he prepared the way for Him. As we reflect on this section of the chapter, are we doing our part to prepare for the second coming of Jesus?

Are we attracting crowds to hear us share the good news? The good news is all about Jesus. Are our presentations whether teaching, preaching, sharing or illustrating about Jesus and His saving grace? John preached and proclaimed that someone more important, some one more special than him with a message that was more important than his would come. In verse 8 of chapter 1 John says,

> *"I indeed baptized you with water: but He shall baptize you with the Holy Ghost".* (KJV)

John baptized Jesus according to verse 9. What is so amazing about the baptism, God spoke from heaven and said, *"Thou are my beloved Son, in whom I am well pleased".* (KJV) Are we living a life that God can say of us that we are His beloved sons and daughters whom He is well pleased? How are we living our lives?

Jesus did not just jump out of the water and began His ministry. He went and tarried in the wilderness for forty days. He needed time to spend with God the Father to prepare Him for His journey He was about to take. Jesus came for a purpose and He needed all of the strength He could get from God the Father. He used that wilderness experience to get closer to

His Father. We all have to use our wilderness experiences. Here is a suggestion; your wilderness experience is your prayer closet. It is that place where it is you and God alone. This is where you pour out your heart, soul and mind to the Master. It is also a place where you listen and let him speak to you.

What is so interesting about this is that there is no box for your wilderness experience. It does not have to be in the church house or at a religious gathering. I often take walks and bike rides by myself. There I find my wilderness experience where God is constantly speaking to me and me to Him. You need that time, that time of you and God away from the everyday trials, tribulations and tests of the world. Watch how God will mold and make you into the vessel that He can use to further the cause of His Glory!

After the time he spent in the wilderness, His prayer and devotional closet, He set out to begin His ministry. Jesus wanted helpers, others to assist with Him in His journey of preaching the gospel. He recruited a group of men. What is so interesting is that they were not Pharisees, Priest, or "church" people. Most of them were not well educated or could command a crowd. Another interesting piece that is so intriguing is that He did not have to spend four to six weeks with them before they could become disciples in His "church". Now do not get me wrong, yes, I do believe in training and getting individuals prepared for the gospel but that does not have to come first. As Mark shares in verses 19 and 20 all Jesus did was tell them to drop what they were doing and follow Him. They did not know everything. They were not familiar with POLICIES PROCESSES and PROCEDURES. They were not familiar with the RULES and REGULATIONS. However, they knew Jesus. They dropped their nets and left their boats to follow Him. They became DISCIPLES and not MEMBERS!

So the question is, are we disciples or members? Do we follow Christ or do we follow our man made ideals of what the church house ought to look like and how we should dress and what kind of music we should play. Membership has its privileges but Discipleship, simply follow the mandates of Jesus Christ. Now that was a shout moment. The prayer of faith is that we all become disciples and not members so that we can just drop our nets and follow Him.

Jesus begins His ministry in town called Capernaum. There Jesus and His disciples attended church. Jesus began to teach in the synagogue. He taught very differently from the priests. Jesus made it plain. Sometimes we can get so caught up in our big words and theological rhetoric that we forget we need to just present the unadulterated gospel of Jesus Christ. In our presentations, sermons, and illustrations are we making it plain or are we trying to impress someone with our eloquent command of the language we speak. To my preachers, are we caught up in our intelligence of our Greek and Hebrew language and dialogue? Let me encourage all of us to make the gospel plain as Jesus did when He taught and spoke. If you want the templet for teaching the gospel study the way Jesus presented it.

When you present the simple truth demons flee. That day Jesus was teaching in the synagogue a man that was demon possessed stood up and said "Leave Us Alone, We Know Who You Are!" The demon or demons eventually left the man. At sound of His name, at the sound of His voice demons must and will flee.

Jesus began His ministry by healing the sick and casting out demons. The lesson taught here is that we need to pay attention to peoples' needs. It is hard to share the word with someone who maybe suffering with sickness or distressed with disease. Sharing the gospel also means we may have to do some tasks outside of giving a bible study, preaching a sermon, holding bible specific seminars. As Jesus healed and helped others people begin to follow Him and listen to His teachings.

Do we find ourselves in our ministries just wanting to preach, teach and then move on? Do we care about those to which God has given their ear to us? When we do, the Church of God will grow in leaps and bounds. People will listen when they know you care. People will listen to the Good News of Jesus Christ!

REFLECTIONS ON MARK 2

JESUS CHRIST, SUPERSTAR

As we venture into Chapter 2 Jesus goes from being a baptismal candidate of John the Baptist to Jesus Christ the superstar. He is now a celebrity.

He returns to Capernaum and the people find out where He is and they begin to gather at the house. Now the Jews were known to go to the synagogue to wait and hear the religious leaders, the priest, scribes and Pharisees to read, preach and interpret the scriptures. However, because of what Jesus had begun with His ministry, they did not wait for Him to come to the synagogue or the church. They went to where He was to hear the word.

Just reflecting on this part of the passage reminds me that I just need to be where Jesus is. The church is not the only place where Jesus is. The church in not the only holy place. The holy place is where we invite the presence of Jesus. Wherever we meet Jesus it becomes holy ground. Whether it is my den, dining room, bedroom or patio. It may be the park or the seashore, but wherever we invite His presence, He is there.

Now don't get it twisted, I do believe in Hebrews 10:25,

"Not forsaking the assembling of ourselves together, as the manner of some is; but exhorting one another: and so much the more, as ye see the day approaching" (KJV).

I believe in coming together to fellowship and worship our Lord in community. I also believe that the church is not the only place to meet Jesus. When you read the book of Acts Chapter 2 the very last verse says,

"…and the Lord added to the church daily such as should be saved" (KJV).

In other words, the newfound church began to invite their neighbors and friends to their homes to share in fellowship and enjoy a meal while also sharing the gospel, the good news. This is how the LORD, added to the church daily. The crowd came to meet Jesus at this house in Capernaum because it was there he shared and taught the gospel.

The crowd was so large that there was a paralytic man who needed and wanted a healing. However, he could not get in due to the gathering. His four companions went on the top of the roof of the house and pulled it open to drop his sick bed in the house in order to get to Jesus. Jesus was so impressed with this man that He first healed him of his sins. That was a shout moment right there. Jesus healed him of his sins, first because He honored the faith of paralytic. The faith of belief is what this paralytic had and the Savior knew it and was moved with compassion. As usual, the "church people" had issues. Just to prove who Jesus was, he then physically healed the man. The crowd was astonished.

Jesus continues in His ministry by calling another disciple. He calls a tax collector, who was despised by the Jews, Matthew. He simply says,

"Follow me. And he arose and followed Him".

When Jesus calls, we must listen. Now Levi Matthew, the tax collector was not very popular with the "church people". However, Jesus called him. He did not know anything or anybody but he knew and recognized who Jesus was. It is not important that you know everything, just need to know Jesus. When you know Jesus, he will teach all that you need to know.

It was obvious to the most casual observer that Jesus was the new Sheriff in town. Jesus' methodology did not line up with the religious leaders' theology, but the Pharisees theology did not line up with the word of God. Their theology focused on policies, procedures and processes rather than on people. The question was asked, "Why don't you fast like us?" This question was asked of Jesus concerning His disciples. Here we go again placing religion in a box. I don't have to do it like you. My experience is different from your experience. Just as we have differing faces, we differ in what needs are. We may also differ in the way we express our faith and have our needs met. There are times when fasting and prayer are needed. There are times when our methodology needs to change. This chapter introduces us to a new Sheriff whose methods do not coincide with those of the religious leaders. As a result, a series of conflicts ensues that will continue throughout Jesus' ministry.

One of my favorite verses in Mark 2 is verse 27,

"And He said unto them, The Sabbath was made for man, and not man for the Sabbath:" (KJV).

Conflict arises once again from the jealousy and envy of the religious leaders. It is so interesting how we can pay attention to others and do not look in the mirror at ourselves. The disciples were walking past a cornfield after leaving the worship experience in the synagogue. As they passed by, they broke off corn to eat. They had not eaten breakfast and they were hungry. When the religious leaders saw this, they approached Jesus. The question arises in verse 24,

"...Behold, why do they on the Sabbath day that which is not lawful?"

Jesus reminds them that it is lawful to do good on the Sabbath. He shares the story of David and his men being hungry and needing to eat. He shared how the High Priest recognized that need and gave them the showbread, which was against the law. Pay attention! The High Priest put people over policy and relationship over religion. The lesson is we must always practice relationship over religion. Relationship will dictate your religion.

The statement that Jesus made in verse 27 is another lesson for us. The Sabbath was made for us. Do not put me in your box. My Sabbath rest may be different from yours. Again, don't get it twisted, we must find ourselves in that rest of reflecting on the creative, redemptive and sustaining power of the Creator. Be mindful that your rest may differ from my rest, but never forget that Sabbath rest should lead us all to the creative and redemptive power of God.

REFLECTIONS ON MARK 3

RELATIONSHIP OVER RELIGION

Jesus continues His ministry. He is back in the synagogue and there is a man with a deformed hand. The bible called it a withered hand. Jesus ask the man to step forward. The religious leaders watched Jesus closely just to see what He would do. Jesus then says in verse 4,

"Is it lawful on the Sabbath to do good or to do evil, to save life or to kill?"

It is interesting that they said stayed silent. Those who sought to trap Him are now silent.

Jesus grieved by the hardness of their hearts, told the man to, *"Stretch out your hand"* vs. 5. The man's hand was healed. It was no longer deformed. The Pharisees, the church people, were angered. They then plotted with the Herodians to destroy Jesus. Did they not recognize who Jesus was? Did they not recognize who He is? These are the church leaders, the teachers and keepers of the scrolls. These are the men that read and taught the predictions of the coming Messiah. They read the prophecies from Isaiah, Jeramiah, Micah and Daniel of how the Christ would come. However, they placed religion over relationship, a themes that will continue throughout the book of Mark. Jesus clearly places relationship over religion when he asked, *"Is it lawful to save life or kill?"* referring back to verse 4. Jesus knows and wants us to recognize that relationship will dictate your religion. He said in John 14:15,

"If you love me keep my commandments" (KJV).

He did not say keep my commandments to love me. It is clear that Jesus has high regard for our relationship with Him. Do we cherish our relationship with Christ? Too many times, we place religion over relationship. Let us move forward by allowing our relationship to lead us to our religion.

Jesus just keeps working His ministry by completing His call of His twelve disciples. His selection had nothing to do with education, social status, religious knowledge or "church position". He simply asked them to drop their "nets" and follow Him. Now they were not all fishermen, but you should get the picture. He did not ask for resumes or how much experience they had. He simply said for them to follow him. When we become followers of Christ, we join a school of "higher" learning that we never graduate from. Why, because we will always be constantly learning from the Master of the universe.

What is the unpardonable sin? The answer to this question is extremely important. Jesus explains that the only sin that will not be forgiven is the one that you will never give up, (see verses 28, 29).

1 John 1:9 says, *"If we confess our sins, He is faithful and just to forgive us our sins, and cleanse us from all unrighteousness"* (KJV).

Not only does He forgive, but He will also cleanse us from all of our bad deeds. This gift is free and all we need to do is just ask. Let's choose now to confess and seek forgiveness as we become sons and daughters of Christ and heirs to the Kingdom of God.

REFLECTIONS ON MARK 4

AN AGRICULTURAL LESSON

Jesus keeps on teaching and sharing. He used stories and examples we call parables. It is amazing how Jesus talked about how the word is spread but also how it is or is not accepted.

We must prepare ourselves to understand that everyone we share the word with will not all respond the same way. People relate differently to what we share and say, even when it is the unadulterated truth. The gospel is that way. In the story that Jesus shares with His disciples he uses the planting of seeds so that they could understand His point. Agriculture, the growing of plants and fruit, was a major economic industry in that time and in that error.

The seed is the gospel and as he tells the story He indicates that some of the seed may fall by the way side and are eaten by the birds. In other words, there is no acceptance. The ground is just not ready to receive the seeds. Some hearts are that way. There are those who are just going to turn a deaf ear to the gospel. They are just not ready to receive or hear the word of God. Have you ever encountered people like that? There is nothing you can do. The seed, the word, cannot grow or be nourished.

Then there are seeds that fell on stony ground and grew up fast. However, there was no substance. There was no nourishment or water. Seeds need to be nourished and watered. However, there is no root as Jesus puts it. Let me put it this way, there is no foundation. We need to be rooted and grounded in the word to keep the enemy at bay. Our study and prayer life needs to be so in tuned that the devil cannot penetrate it. This will not stop his attacks but it will sure make it is very difficult to penetrate and take our hearts from the true life giver. To be a true disciple of Christ, and to have a strong relationship, one He desires requires us to be rooted and grounded in His word. This calls for a true sincere devotional life through prayer and study of His word.

He continues with the seed sown among the thorns. They do believe but when the first thing comes that offends or disrupts their comfort level they become as Mark pens, unfruitful. Now we must understand what fruitful means. Fruitful simply means, producing goods or helpful results;

in other words, being productive. As a disciple of Christ we are to be fruitful or productive in our passion to share His love and saving grace. Unfruitful means we no longer have that urgency or that passion to spread the good news or the gospel of Jesus Christ. What also happens is that where these seeds are sown the thorns choke them out; Verse 19,

> *"And the cares of this world, and the deceitfulness of riches, and the lusts of other things entering in, choke the word, and it becometh unfruitful"* (KJV). Matthew 6:24 says, *"No man can serve two masters: for either he will hate the one, and love the other; or else he will hold to the one, and despise the other. Ye cannot serve God and mammon"* (KJV).

We must never let the pleasures of this world cause us to lose our connection with the Master of the universe.

His last example in this story is the crescendo of the story. This is where the seeds are sown on good ground. In other words on those who readily receive the word and not only keeps it themselves, but as we do daily with good news, share it. In other words they become fruitful, some more than others, but fruitful or productive. They spread the word with an urgency and passion because of what Christ has done in their lives. This is where we need to be. We need to share what Christ has given us and use all of our being to live the life so that others may see a reflection of Christ in us.

Jesus continues to speak about the Kingdom of God; again, comparing it to fruit being planted and grown. In the agriculture world, this process must lead to a great harvest, as that is how the farmer makes his living. He is looking for a great harvest. He goes in with the sickle and takes out all of the bad weed and grass that has attempted to ruin the crop.

Are you glad the salvation is a process? Verses 28 – 29 explain the process. This is what it says,

> *"For the earth bringeth forth fruit of herself, first the blade, then the ear, after that the full corn in the ear"* (KJV).

It's a process. You grow in faith. As you grow you get a little stronger and stronger. You, through the power of the Holy Spirit, overcome the obstacles, overcome the wiles of the devil and now you await the great harvest of the life giver. As you read this, it's a shout moment!

As Jesus shared many stories that day, He grew weary and needed a break from the crowd. He thought to go to the other side of the lake. When a storm came up the winds and waves knocking against the boat. That's how the enemy operates. The minute you believe and think you are secure, here he comes. This time he was coming against the Master of the universe. Only the creator and controller of nature itself could simply say to the wind, verse 39, "...*Peace, be still. And the wind ceased, and there was a great calm*" (KJV). So as they said one to another, what manner of man is this that nature, wind and sea obey His voice. Only the Master, Creator could cause nature to obey His voice. Can we follow the winds and the sea and obey His voice.

REFLECTIONS ON MARK 5

WHO TOUCHED MY CLOTHES?

The Master's work is never done. He is amazing. He just ordered the wind and the waves to obey His command and now as He travels to the other side of the lake; He is confronted with who else but the devil with company. What is so amazing about this account is that the demons in this man knew Jesus. The man was possessed, and the demons spoke through this man. Verse 7 states,

> "And he cried out with a loud voice and said, What have I to do with You, Jesus, Son of the Most High God? I implore You by God that You do not torment me" (KJV).

Do we really recognize Jesus in our lives? Can we say we know who He is? We need to quit ignoring the obvious and recognize Jesus in our lives. Worship Him not for what He does for us, no; worship Him for who He is. Exodus 20:11 says,

> "For in six days the Lord made the heavens and the earth, the sea and all that in them is...". Revelation 14:7 says, "...and worship Him who made heaven and earth, and the sea, and the fountains of waters" (KJV).

Again, we worship Him for who He is. Who is He, He is our Creator. You can pause at this point and take a praise break because this is also a shout moment.

I am so glad that He commanded the demons to flee. That is what He does with our sins when we confess, He forgives and makes us clean. Do you not want to be in relationship with the Son of the Most High God? Because when you are, you will give Him the glory He deserves, and you will share and tell everybody about His love and saving grace.

As I reflect on this chapter, I cannot help but think about how Jesus' work was never done. Here is one of the synagogue's leaders, maybe the head elder, daughter is very ill and needs Jesus. Remember as Jesus has begun His ministry it appears that the synagogue was becoming empty and where Jesus was, there was an overflow. As we have said before, teaching, healing and worship does not necessarily have to happen in the synagogue. Let me get in your yard, or at the church house. Here is a religious leader leaving possibly His post to seek Jesus for healing. He knew who Jesus was.

However, the crowd is so heavy with all kinds of people needing healing, needing to hear what God must teach, and needing salvation. Just wanting to be witnesses to what was transpiring when a woman who had been suffering for many years needing relief from her infirmity. This ailment had haunted her for 12 years. She had an issue of blood as the bible states. She was suffering all this time and just needed a healing. The crowd was so large that she could not get through. Do we allow ourselves to place religion over relationship so that those who need Jesus we block their approach? This is going to get radical but that is what we do when people mess up or sin. We send them away to get right. In other words, we tell them you must leave the church for a period of time and come back when you get it right. That compares to telling a gunshot victim when they come to the hospital to go home and come back when you stop the bleeding. This is an oxymoron. When we need the most help that is the time, we need to be close to Jesus.

Despite the crowd, she wants relief. She has urgency about herself and she is determined to get to Jesus. What an example of the urgency and passion to get to the Master! She so believed that Jesus could heal her she says in verse 28,

"...If I may touch but His clothes, I shall be whole" (KJV).

What faith to believe, if I can just touch His clothes, I will be healed. Her faith is what healed her. No doctor visit, no medication, no medical consultation just belief that just by touching not Him but something that was in contact with Him would make her whole. Despite the crowd, Jesus felt her touch His clothes and said in verse 30, *"...who touched my clothes?"* (KJV). It was her un-denying faith in just believing in the healing power of Jesus. All of this going on while on His way to heal the religious leader's daughter.

It is strange that He did not seek healing at the synagogue, but he sought Jesus. By the time Jesus arrives, Jairus' daughter is dead. The people and family are grieving the lost. Jesus simply tells them in verse 39,

> *"...Why make this commotion and weep? The damsel is not dead, but sleepeth"* (KJV).

However, unlike the woman with the issue of blood, they did not believe. Jesus had all the unbelievers to leave. He did not need any doubters in there. He needed spiritual unity of the right mind and spirit. Psalms 133:1 state, *"Behold, how good and how pleasant it is for brethren to dwell together in unity!"* (KJV). At times to move the Holy Spirit we need unity. Pentecost brought on unity. When you come together pray and believe supernatural experiences will take place in our lives. This is what happens. The child is awakened by the Master. Why, because unity was there. At that moment in that house, it was pleasant for the brethren to dwell together in unity.

Jesus' ministry continues to grow as people are healed. People are encouraged. Sins are being forgiven. It is exciting times among the people of God. Let us all get excited about Jesus and who He is.

REFLECTIONS ON MARK 6

OPPORTUNITIES TO RECEIVE

Jesus returns to Nazareth, His beginnings, the place where He was from. He began to teach and share and many marveled at His teachings and wondered where He got these things. On the other hand, they knew who He was as to His earthly beginnings and even brought up His background. At this point, they did not want to hear Him.

Have you ever wondered why the hardest people to reach or the closest to our hearts? Not all but most friends and relatives never see you as an instrument for the Lord. As Peter puts it in the Message Bible Translation, I Peter 2:9-10

"But you are the ones chosen by God, chosen for the high calling of priestly work, chosen to be a holy people, God's instruments to do His work and speak out for Him, to tell others of the night and day difference He made for you from nothing to something, from rejected to accepted".

God has called us all to the "Priestly Work". It doesn't matter if you are a theology major or never finished high school. Once you become a follower and believer of Christ, you are anointed for the "Priestly Work". Sometimes those who are close to us, family and neighbors, teammates and classmates, siblings and cousins, let's not forget husbands and wives, have hard times seeing us in our "Priestly Work". As we teach and share, they may see our mistakes and misfortunes our disasters and dilemmas of life. They may dwell on our valley experiences as opposed to our mountain top victories. All of this at times makes it hard to accept our calling to go ye, therefore.

My encouragement is not to become discouraged or dismayed. This would make the devil oh so happy. The book of James says in James 4:7,

"Submit yourselves therefore to God. Resist the devil, and he will flee" (KJV).

This is not just from temptation of sin but also the temptation of doubt and discouragement. It is not our job to reap the harvest. Our job is to plant the seed. The bible says that in Romans 2:4,

"Or despises thou the riches of His goodness and forbearance and longsuffering; not knowing that the goodness of God leadeth thee to repentance?" (KJV).

It is God's goodness through the power of His Holy Spirit that leads us to repentance. So, go tell and teach. Then go tell and teach again and again and again. Then watch the goodness of God lead even your closest family and friends to Christ.

As we teach and share, we need to make disciples. We teach, share and train at the same time. The goal is to prepare others and ourselves for the Kingdom of Christ. We do that by having urgency and a passion to share the good news. The good news is the gospel of Jesus Christ. The good news is found in John 3:16,

> *"For God so loved the world that He gave His only begotten Son, that whosoever believeth in Him should not perish but have everlasting life"* (KJV).

The good news is found in Romans 5:8,

> *"…While we were yet sinners Christ died for us"* (KJV).

Our calling is to offer the free gift that God has to offer and that is the sacrifice of His Son, Jesus Christ. You teach, share, and make disciples. Not everyone will accept your presentations no matter how eloquent you present or how much passion you relate. However, your job is to plant and keep moving. It is the opportunities that individuals have been given. Ultimately it will be their choice, not because you were ineffective. It will be because they did not yield to the unction of the Holy Spirit. Revelation 3:20 says,

> *"Behold, I stand at the door and knock: if any man hear my voice, and open the door, I will come in to him, and will sup with him, and he with me" (KJV).*

We are to introduce Christ. Now it is up to those who receive the opportunity to decide to follow Jesus all the way.

We must share the good news even if it costs us our life. John the Baptist preached the truth and it cost him his life. Yet Jesus said in Luke 7:28,

> *"For I say unto you, Among those that are born of women there is not a greater prophet than John the Baptist: but he that is least in the kingdom of God is greater than he"* (KJV).

Despite the doubters and the Pharisees constant criticisms Jesus kept on teaching, preaching and performing miracles that marveled the thousands that followed, heard and witnessed what they saw. Jesus is still working miracles in our lives today. You may not have been the benefactor of the five loaves and two fish. You may not have been on the sea when He walked on the water. Nevertheless, you have a story. What is your story, what is your testimony?

REFLECTIONS ON MARK 7

TRADITIONS OR BIBLICAL PRINCIPLES, NOW THAT IS THE QUESTION

Once again, the Pharisees confront Jesus. Church people can be so caught up in the rituals and traditions that they forget about people. In this chapter, they are confronting Jesus on why the disciples are breaking bread with unwashed hands; even saying that this is a "tradition" of the elders to wash hands before breaking bread. And the question is asked, "Really"?

Do we hold traditions and rituals over people in need? Once again and this has been mentioned as I reflect on this book we must not put policies, procedures and processes over people. There are times that not only church pew people, but church leaders tend to place people last. I am so glad that Jesus never placed rituals and traditions over people. I will quote the same text He did from Isaiah 29:13,

> *"Wherefore the Lord said, Forasmuch as this people draw near me with their mouth, and with their lips do honour me, but have removed their heart far from me, and their fear toward me is taught by the precept of men:"* (KJV).

We get caught up in traditions and rituals. We get caught up in making sure we are dressed the correct way, that we are saying the right denominational slangs, that we are singing the "correct" hymns, that we are eating and drinking correctly, that we reverence a building with pews, chairs, pulpits, communion tables, choir lofts and instruments. Just to be clear, there is no dress code in the bible. Now let's not get it twisted. We should present ourselves the best we can when we come to meet Jesus at His house of worship. However, if I decide not to wear a coat and tie or my wife or daughters decide to wear pants and no hosiery the pits of hell will not prevail in their lives. The same is true of denominational slangs, songs and hymns. Jesus is not coming to save you because you speak a certain religious or denominational slang or because you sing certain "denominational hymns". Jesus is coming to save those who accept His gift and His gift is not defined by a denomination. It is defined by those who accept the free gift of Jesus Christ which will lead them to the true remnant church of Revelation 12:17; which simply tells us that the remnant churches keeps the commandments of God, all of them, and have the testimony of Jesus Christ.

We continue to reverence a building. God instructed Moses to build a sanctuary that He may dwell among His people. The whole sanctuary message is to lead us back to the "Most Holy Place", which is in the very presence of God, the Eden experience that God intended for us to enjoy. The sanctuary pointed to Christ and the sacrificial love that He would show by dying in our stead. When He died, the curtain in the sanctuary dividing the Holy Place from the Most Holy Place, split from top to bottom indicating that now we can come as the Hebrew writer says in Hebrews 4:16, "Let us therefore come boldly unto the throne of grace, that we may obtain mercy, and find grace to help in the time of need" (KJV). In other words, I don't need a church house to go directly to Jesus. I don't need a priest, pastor, bishop or deacon. I can go directly to Him because Jesus paid it all.

Let's not let rituals and traditions, policies, processes and procedures separate us from the love of Jesus Christ. Paul said it in Romans 8:38-39,

> *"For I am persuaded, that neither death, nor life, nor angels, nor principalities, nor powers, nor things present, nor things to come. Nor height, nor depth, not any other creature, shall be able to separate us from the love of God, which is in Christ Jesus our Lord"* (KJV).

In other words, not even rituals or traditions will separate me from my Savior.

REFLECTIONS ON MARK 8

WHO WANTS A HAPPY MEAL?

Jesus is doing what Jesus does. He sees a need and responds to the need. This crowd had followed Him for three days. They had not eaten. They were hungry. Jesus satisfied that need and had plenty of leftovers.

We all need physical food to survive. There is no doubt that after three days of not eating the people, the crowd, were hungry. They needed to eat, and Jesus fed them. However, Jesus did something else they needed during those three days. He fed them spiritually.

Jesus has plenty of spiritual nourishment for us with plenty of leftovers. We cannot survive without spiritual food. If we are to stay connected to Christ, we must feast on His spiritual nourishment. We can survive days without physical food, but we need spiritual food daily. Jesus said it Himself when He taught the disciples how to pray in Matthew 6:11,

"Give us this day our daily bread" (KJV).

We should daily ask Jesus to give us what we need that day. Every day is a new level. For every new level, there is a new devil. That means it is important that we feast on Jesus' spiritual nourishment daily. Do not worry about Jesus running out. I can promise you He has plenty of leftovers.

Spiritual nourishment helps us to see. Our physical eyesight may be good but what about our spiritual eyesight. Do we need a miracle to clear our way? Do we need to be physically knocked down to realize who Jesus is? When we are knocked down, do we realize we are in need of a Savior just as the blind man in Bethsaida? Spiritual nourishment will help us see Jesus and recognize who He is. This will also help us to recognize the miracles that Jesus performs in our lives without question.

Despite the miracles, healings, teachings and assisting those in need with other needs, Jesus came to this earth for one reason and one reason only. He came for our salvation. He came to take our place so that we could have His place. Before He died, there were those who were close to Him who did not accept that fact. But Isaiah 53:5 says,

"But He was wounded for our transgressions, He was bruised for our iniquities: the chastisement of our peace was upon Him; and with His stripes we are healed (KJV).

He suffered and died so that we might have a right to the tree of life.

I am so glad for His sacrifice and love that gives us a chance to finally enjoy that Eden experience He meant for us to have at creation before the fall of our first parents. Before we do and because of sin, there are some crosses that we must bear. Sometimes that means to stand alone. Sometimes that means we may have to shun the world. Mark 8:36-37, (KJV), ask the following two questions:

v. 36 – *"For what shall it profit a man, if he shall gain the whole world, and lose his own soul?"*

v. 37 – *"Or what shall a man give in exchange for his soul?"*

Let's not be ashamed of the gospel in this sinful generation. Let's choose Jesus over the pleasures of the world.

REFLECTIONS ON MARK 9

WHO IS AN UNBELIEVER?

Mark Chapter 9 begins with Jesus on the Mount of Transfiguration. Jesus was transfigured. As He gets close to His goal, His reason for coming the first time, He needed some reassurance and encouragement.

There are times when we need reassurance and encouragement that we are on the right path. As we take our Christian journey, our walk of faith we truly need encouragement. The reason being is found in Matthew 7:14 which says,

> *"Because strait is the gate, and narrow is the way, which leadeth unto life, and few there that find it"* (KJV).

There are all kinds of Pastors, Teachers, Bishops, and Faith Based Leaders who seek to confuse and confound what people believe. In fact, in that same chapter, 7, of Matthew, verse 15 says,

> *"Beware of false prophets, which come to you in sheep's clothing, but inwardly they are ravening wolves"* (KJV).

As children of the Most High God, we need reassuring and encouragement as we take this faithful journey.

So, God the Father sent God the son some encouragement with two faithful servants in Elijah and Moses. This was just to encourage Him and to hold Him up and let Him know that this was the only way for mankind to ever enjoy that Eden experience that God intended from the very beginning. What a wonder that Jesus gave up glory to save us, to redeem us, and to deliver us from the vice grips of the devil. What love from our Master and Creator.

If only we would believe in Him. It's our unbelief that keeps us from growing in the faith. As we go through this chapter, there is a boy who needs to be healed. He is demon possessed. But there were unbelievers. As we have discussed and will discuss throughout this book Jesus healed people almost daily. This healing power He had given it to the Disciples. However, they could not heal this boy.

As we take our journey through faith there will be bumps and bruises along the way. There will be difficulties as well as disappointments but we must never let our faith waiver. It was the unbelief that kept this boy from being healed. The boy was being controlled by a demon and the disciples could not heal him. Could it be that the disciples lacked faith in the power Jesus had given them? Could it be the people gathered and the family lacked faith? Jesus in verse 19 simply says, and I love how the Clear Word Bible states it,

> *"You people have such little faith! How much longer do I have to keep teaching you? How much longer do I have to be patient with you? Bring the boy here"* (KJV).

This is the climax of this event. This situation with this demon in this boy had been going on for quite some time. Jesus lets the father know that if he has enough faith anything is possible. That is so true in all of our lives. If we have enough faith in Christ, anything is possible. Paul penned it quite eloquently when in Philippians 4:13 he wrote,

> *"I can do all things through Christ which strengtheneth me"* (KJV).

This text along should cause a praise break. I know you are reading this book, but it is okay to have shout moment because we can truly do all things though Christ who gives us the strength and encouragement to move forward. We must ask Jesus daily for us to have the courage and strength to believe more and more in His promises because His word is true.

We get this belief through earnest and a dedicated sincere prayer and fasting life. This is how we stay connected and charged. This will allow us to have that peace that passes all understanding; peace even in the middle of your valley experiences. Staying connected will give you that peace. I can testify that I am not only a witness but a recipient of that peace. Remember the key is to stay connected to Christ.

Staying connected and charged to Christ will not let us get caught up in who is the greatest or who is in charge. Jesus apparently walks in on a conversation in verses 33-34 where the disciples are discussing their position of authority when Jesus would become King. Staying connected takes those thoughts and pursuits out of your spirit. First and most importantly Jesus did not come the first time to establish an earthly kingdom. His assignment was to redeem fallen mankind, to make atonement for mankind's rebellion. He came to guarantee my salvation. It does not matter what my position is or if I am number one or the very last to get in the kingdom. I just want to get there, how about you?

We also need to be careful who we think is getting there. We need to be careful especially with denominations. In verse 38, as I reflect, John made this statement to Jesus,

> *"And John answered Him, saying, Master, we saw one casting out devils in thy name, and he followeth not us: and we forbad him, because he followeth not us"* (KJV).

Jesus simply answered John by telling him in verse 40,

> *"For he that is not against us is on our part"* (KJV).

In other words, if he is preaching the gospel, the good news of Jesus Christ he is on our side. This is so profound as we tackle the text in II Corinthians 6:14,

> *"Be ye not unequally yoked together with unbelievers: for what fellowship hath righteousness with unrighteousness? and what communion hath light with darkness? And what concord hath Christ with Belial? Or what part hath he that believeth with an infidel?"* (KJV).

This unbelief has nothing to do with denomination or what church you attend. An unbeliever is an infidel. An infidel by definition is not accepting any faith or especially Christianity. An infidel or an unbeliever is one who does not believe in God or the bible. There are many people in different denominations who believe in God. They may not have accepted all of the biblical teachings but the one common practice they do have is they believe in God. So how do you call anyone an infidel who believe in God? John 10:16 is very clear when Jesus said and I quote, "

> *And other sheep I have, which are not of this fold: them also I must bring, and they shall hear my voice; and there shall be one fold, and one shepherd"* (KJV).

What this is saying is that Jesus recognizes that there are those who believe in Him and not one of them. They are not an infidel. If they are for Jesus, they are not against Jesus. I believe at the appointed time He will bring them to Him as they hear His voice. Let's quit making denominations exclusive clubs for "members" only. Sounds like the American Express commercial. That's why I preach Jesus and when genuine people accept Jesus, they will know what church or denomination to be a part of.

There is a man who attends my church. He participates in our worship experiences every Saturday, including what we call Sabbath School, which is bible study. He is there religiously every Saturday. He returns a faithful tithe and offering every week. I have approached him a few times about becoming a disciple. Just as a side bar, we believe in discipleship and not membership. But he always declines. I can declare that this man is not an infidel. He loves God and believes in the Ten Commandments and the testimony of Jesus Christ. As the bible says, at the appointed time he will hear the voice of Jesus. I repeat as Jesus did, if he is for us then he is not against us.

REFLECTIONS ON MARK 10

ALL IN THE FAMILY

This chapter begins with family. God installed two institutions at creation, the Sabbath and Marriage.

It is not surprising to me that these two institutions are the very ones the devil attacks the most. It is clear that God intended marriage to be forever, and man nor woman should seek divorce just because they want to marry someone else. This is a sacred union and before you go into it, much prayer and fasting should be undertaken for the Holy Spirit to direct you to the right one. To God be the glory when you allow the Holy Spirit to direct you to that person. I can truly testify that the Holy Spirit directed me to my wife of 42 years. Don't want anybody else and I am not looking for anybody else. Our relationship was setup by the Holy Spirit. Don't get it twisted we have had some bad days and valley experiences, that's life, but we have endured the journey and that is Christ.

As family matures and grows there are the children. As a matter of fact, the bible tells us in Psalms 127:3,

> *"Lo, children are an heritage of the Lord: and the fruit of the womb is His reward"* (KJV).

Children are an heritage of the Lord. In other words, they are an inheritance. These precious beings are gifts from God. Jesus loved children. In verses 13 – 16 the disciples attempt to run the children off, but Jesus said bring them to me because He enjoyed their company. Children are very trust worthy. That's how we must be to inherit eternal life. We must come as a little child ever trusting in the word of God and ever eager to continue to hear and most importantly to obey is voice.

Family is about love. Jesus said in John 14:15,

> *"If you love me, keep my commandments"* (KJV).

We just can't keep the commandments because the church says so or we want to be a part of some movement. Keeping the commandments should be out of love, respect and adoration for our Creator. Love is not an emotion it is a state of being. It defines a true relationship. When you love, you give. When you love, you sacrifice. As I reflect on the rich young ruler, he kept the commandments, but he did not love.

Jesus declared in the gospel according to Matthew that all 10 commandments rest on these two. Look at what Matthew 22:37-40 says,

> *"Jesus said unto him, Thou shalt love the Lord thy God with all thy heart, and with all thy soul, and with all thy mind. This is the first and great commandment. And the second is like unto it, Thou shalt love thy neighbor as thyself. On these two commandments hang all the law and the prophets"* (KJV).

Love is the foundation of our relationship with the Savior. It is this love that leads you to sacrifice and to the giving or all to save another. As I reflect on the rich young ruler, I have to ask the question, how many of us are like the rich young ruler? We go to church. We keep the commandments. However, our careers, our homes, our cars, our families come before God. We keep the commandments as long as they don't make us uncomfortable or take us out our personal comfort zone. Let's not be like the rich young ruler. Let's love the Lord our God with all of heart, mind and soul; as well as our neighbor, as our self.

In verses 32-34 Jesus shares with family that when they go to Jerusalem the church people will turn against Him. Keep in mind that this is all part of the process of paying the price for our sins. He is setting Himself up to take what we deserve so that we can get what He deserves. We deserve death. The bible says in Romans 6:23,

> *"For the wages of sin is death; but the gift of God is eternal life through Jesus Christ our Lord"* (KJV).

So, He died for us. He suffered for us. He was scorned for us. This is the best part. Not only did He die for us but here is the climax, here is what has scared the devil to his rage - Jesus rose! He was resurrected. He died on Friday and arose on Sunday. What a Mighty God We Serve!

REFLECTIONS ON MARK 11

MARDI GRAS IN JERUSALEM

When I reflect on the first part of this chapter, I can't help but shout when I see Jesus is the center of a parade. We like to call that day Palm Sunday because as Jesus rode, the crowd laid down palm tree branches, which are very leafy and spread them on the road. It is good to acknowledge our leaders. Now Jesus was not a politician of that time. He was not a king, governor or senator. In the Jewish religious world, He was not a Scribe, Levite, Pharisee or Priest. However, His works paved the way for this attention. I once had a former supervisor tell me, as I climbed the ladder of success with the Louisiana Department of Children and Family Services, to let my work ethics lead my way. I listened to that advice and it did affect my career in a positive way. All Jesus did was teach, preach, heal the sick, feed the hungry, and raise the dead. He never asked for a "church" position, but His ministry was a success throughout Judea.

When we just do the work of the Lord. We will reap the reward. We must always realize that the reward may not always happen in this life. John the Baptist is a prime example. He was raised for the simple purpose of preparing the way for Jesus' first coming. He preached so hard that he had a huge following. There were some who believed his word and some who just thought he was crazy. He even baptized Jesus. Then he went to prison and was beheaded. But Jesus said in Luke 7:28,

> *"For I say unto you, Among those that are born of women there is not a greater prophet than John the Baptist."*

John will realize his reward when Jesus comes the second time. Our reward, our parade does happen. We just do not always realize that. I lost what I thought was my dream job that I had worked so hard for. I thought the bottom fell out. I was not in the valley, but under the valley. My career gone, taken away. But God! A year later, I was called to pastor a small congregation in Slidell Louisiana. Don't ask, I know you never heard of it. It is a small town on the north shore of Lake Ponchatrain about 25 miles north east of New Orleans. I have never been so fulfilled in all my life. It was at that time that I realized God's purpose for my life. To teach and preach the gospel of Jesus Christ. We need to begin to realize that God's purpose for our life is our earthly reward. Pray that the Holy Spirit leads you to your true purpose.

The parade and accolades would be short lived as a few days later Jesus comes to the temple and observes what is taking place. He became angry. Yes, Jesus became angry. The bible says in Ephesians 4:26, *"Be ye angry, and sin not.* Jesus became angry and as this chapter indicates, He even turned the tables over and made this statement in Mark 11:17,

> *"And He taught, saying unto them, Is it not written, My house shall be called of all nations the house of prayer? but ye have made it a den of thieves"* (KJV).

Our first thought as we process this verse is that they were in there making money and profit at the expense of the congregants. Yes, they were, but as I reflect, there were also some other things going on as well. Not only was it a money thing, but the church leaders begin to practice "traditions" that they soon began to teach as biblical principles.

The "church" has come up with a dress code. The church has come up with a form of worship that is tailored and fashioned after a certain ethnic group or culture. This is across all religions. We have "traditions" and "practices" that we have implemented in all religions that have nothing to do with biblical principles that move us to salvation. Let me give you a prime example. The unwed pregnant young lady. We immediately ask that she submit a letter and have her name removed from the roll or be subject to a "board and business meeting" where her name will be voted to be removed. In some churches they even have the young lady to stand before the church and confess her wrong. Salvation by works at its best. There is nothing biblical about that. In fact, when Jesus was approached about the woman caught in adultery, He forgave her and simply told her to go and sin no more. Please go and read the account in John 8:1-11. Our confessions of sin and wrongdoings is to be presented to God and God alone. David in his prayer of confession puts it this way in Psalms 51:4,

> *"Against thee, thee only, have I sinned, and done this evil in thy sight: that thou mightiest be justified when thou speakest, and be clear when thou judgest"* (KJV).

Our sins and rebellion are all against God. When we confess and God forgives, it is the power of the Holy Spirit that will lead you to the person or persons you need to go to.

Even in our worship "traditions" and "practices", we condemn worship styles because we were "taught" to worship a certain way. Let me suggest to you that your worship and worship style is based on your relationship with God and how you express that relationship based on your culture. For many years, we were told that playing drums and guitars in church was a "sin". However, when you read Psalms we are encouraged to praise the Lord with all forms of instruments. In Psalms 150:5 it states,

> *"Praise Him upon the loud symbols: praise hymn upon high sounding symbols"* (KJV).

Heaven will be full of music and holy noise. As a good friend of mine always says, we must practice kingdom living down here so that we will be able to enjoy up there. Let us not turn our preferences and practices into biblical principles.

How do we get out of our traditions and unbiblical practices? Through our sincere devotional life. We must keep a song in our heart and a prayer on our lips. In verse 25 Jesus says when we pray, if there is something between someone and us, we must forgive. Notice He does not say only if you are the guilty party - even if you were the offended. Forgiveness is the key to opening up the portals of heaven. In Mark 11:25 Jesus said,

> *"And when ye stand praying, forgive, if ye have ought against any: that your Father also which is in heaven may forgive your trespasses"* (KJV).

In other words, God will not forgive you if you can't forgive others. Jesus set the bar. We are to forgive others as Jesus forgives us. Let's keep the portals of heaven open. We need to stay connected and committed to Christ.

REFLECTIONS ON MARK 12

TRICK OR TREAT

As my mind reflects on the first part of this chapter I cannot help but to think about rejection and what this means. Jesus takes the time to tell this parable. Keep in mind that parables were teaching moments and were intentionally directed to the audience in attendance. Some of the attendees were priests and the leaders of the "church". Verse 12 sums up the feelings of the priests and leaders when it says,

> *"And they sought to lay hold on him, but feared the people: for they knew that He had spoken the parable against them: and they left Him, and went their way"* (KJV).

What is so interesting about this parable is the fact that not only did they reject the servants as well as the son, but they also sought to do them and in some instances harm even unto death. We have tendencies to disagree with one another to the point that we become disagreeable. We get angry, which is okay, but then we sin. This particular issue is of a higher value then even this. This particular issue deals with their rejection of Jesus. They knew it and this is why they sought to lay hold on Him or to do Him harm. They knew He was correct and they could do nothing at the time to stop Him.

Let me carry this to another level. When you come into knowledge of truth a change should come. Let me suggest that this change could be a total embracement of truth or a total rejection of truth. Life is all about choices. *"...choose you this day whom ye will serve..."* according to Joshua 24:15. Be careful what and whom you reject. As Jesus reminded them of the story of the stone that the builders rejected. It was that corner stone that just kept being tossed aside or thrown away. That stone was different. It was not shaped liked the other stones. It did not look like the other stones. It was peculiar. Do you know that word? At the end of the day, it was just the stone the builders needed to uphold the foundation of the building. My encouragement is that we hold on to the stone that the builders rejected, the carpenter's son, Mary's baby, the teacher who had no degree, the preacher who wasn't a known theologian. He was not a Pharisee, Scribe, or Priest. He was Jesus, the stone that the builders rejected. Let us not do as the builders did, let's embrace Jesus!

The leaders and the priests were angry and sought to do Him harm, but He was popular with the people so they dare not turn the people against them. They were already angry about the temple issue. You remember, when Jesus came to the temple and turned tables over because they were taking advantage of the congregants by not only stealing, but setting up man made policies, processes and procedures that had nothing to do with worship or salvation. In their eyes Jesus was a marked man. So, they attempted once again to try and "trick" Him into saying something against the law.

Now this trick question comes from the conversation being held in verses 13 – 17 of our chapter. Here is the question in verse 14,

> *"...Master, we know that thou art true, and carest for no man:*
> *for thou regardest not the person of men, but teachest the way of*
> *God in truth: Is it lawful to give tribute to Caesar, or not?"*

I love the way they used Satan's tactics as He did to Eve, very subtle. They attempted to flatter Him. Here is what The Clear Word Bible says in verses 14 - 15,

> *"...Teacher we know that You're honest and teach the truth. Do*
> *you think it is right for us to pay taxes to a foreign government?*
> *What do you think we should do?"*

Jesus replied, "Why are you trying to trick Me? Do you have a Roman coin? Let me see it". Once again, Jesus exposes them for who they were with the question, why are you trying to trick me. His answer astonished them when He used that coin to say give to Caesar what is due him and to God what is due to Him. They had nothing to say after that.

Part of the devil's arsenal is to use "trickery and flattery". Back in the day, if I can use this term, there was an Amazing Facts Bible Study Guide named "Don't Be Fooled". Let me just reemphasize that title. Don't be fooled. The devil wants to trick you by using flattery. He did it to Eve and he used all of the ways he could muster to do it to Jesus. But unlike Eve, stand firm and unmovable, always abiding in the word of God.

If we would just abide in His word and follow His commandments, we can have a chance. As we reflect on this portion of the chapter, let's keep in mind that all Pharisees and Scribes were not bad. When this one scribe asked Jesus this in verse 28, *"... Which is the first commandment of all?"* As we know there are 10 commandments, but throughout the gospels Jesus summarizes the 10 into two; verse 30,

> *"And thou shalt love the Lord thy God with all thy heart, and with all thy soul, and with all thy mind, and with all thy strength: this is the first commandment"* (KJV) and verse 31, *"And the second is like, namely this, Thou shalt love thy neighbor as thyself. There is no other commandment greater than these"* (KJV).

Even the commandments are based on love. The first four demonstrate our love for God and the second six demonstrate our love for each other. Love is the machine that drives us to salvation. Love is the machine the drives us to one another. John 3:16, *"For God so loved the world that He gave His only begotten Son..."* All we have to do is believe, accept and love. What a mighty God!

It is interesting, what we love, we resource. As I reflect on the last four verses of this chapter, I just think about my true reason for giving. I know you are familiar with this story. Jesus, observing in the sanctuary, notices the many who were putting money into the treasury. Plenty of these people were rich and well off. It's in the text, *"...and many that were rich cast in much..."* (verse 41, KJV). From His observation, those giving did not return sacrificially. Oh, they gave in abundance, but it was not through sacrifice. In our time, we would call it a write off. I am not sure if they had that process back there, however, they were not giving from the heart. Again, what you love, you resource, no matter what the cost or sacrifice.

Yes, I am going there. We should return a faithful tithe and offering. Malachi 3:10 tells us to

> *"Bring ye all the tithes into the storehouse, that there may be meat in mine hours, and prove me now herewith, saith the Lord of hosts, if I will not open you the windows of heaven, and pour you out a blessing, that there shall not be room enough to receive it" (KJV). The widow's two mites were much more than what all the rich people had given.* This is what Jesus said in verses 43 – 44, *"...Verily I say unto you, That this poor widow hath cast more in, than all they which have cast into the treasury: For all they did cast in of their abundance; but she of her want did cast in all that she had, even all her living" (KJV).* She gave her all. My question to you, are you giving your all?

REFLECTIONS ON MARK 13

WHAT'S GOING TO HAPPEN?

The word of God is full of prophecy and end time signs. The gospel according to Mark is no different. Here in chapter 13 the disciples ask Jesus to tell them about the signs of the end and when they will be. In this chapter, Jesus mentions several issues and signs. As I reflect on this chapter, Jesus knows that His time is getting short. The reason for His first appearance was vastly approaching. He began to share with them the signs.

The very first thing that He warned them against was to be careful and not be deceived. Verse 5, *"...Take heed less any man deceive you"*. The very reason we find ourselves in this sinful condition is the fact that the devil deceived Eve. It was the art of deception that convinced Eve to rebel against the Most High God. He goes on to tell them that many would come in His name. In other words, there will be false prophets speaking false prophecy that ultimately leads one to rebel against God. Isn't that what happened to Eve? You remember the story, Satan tells her that, *"...Ye shall not surely die..."* according to Genesis 3:4. Well, eventually Eve did die along with the many descendants from her and Adam, all the way down to us. I am 62 years old. I cannot count the number of funerals that I have attended or officiated.

He spoke about wars and rumors of wars. If you are not aware of this, you are both blind and deaf with no realization of reality. We live in the midst of this daily. There is war going on somewhere and with the emergence of nuclear warfare, the rumors of war are steady mounting.

We see the times all around us. Even families betraying families. Children rising up against parents. Parents abandoning children. Foster care cases are at an all-time high as so-called parents are either abandoning their children or abusing them to the point that they can no longer take care of them. Again, signs of the time!

Religious freedoms are being slowly withdrawn. The separation of church and state is rapidly disappearing. Religious organizations that are not necessarily following Christianity are being attacked. Mosque and Jewish Temples have been the target of attacks. Those of the Islamic faith are considered terrorist and extremist. All of this in the name of religion. Here is a prime example of Religion over Relationship. So the question is, who is next or what denomination or faith based organization is next? One of Jesus' predictions is that those who follow Him will be delivered up to councils or those in authority. All for the sake of Christ. That time is coming!

Jesus also in this chapter predicted the rise of false prophets. Verse 22 states,

> *"For false Christs and false prophets shall rise, and shall shew signs and wonders, to seduce, if it were possible, even the elect"*, (kjv).

Jesus give this warning to warn us and to keep us on guard. As I reflect on this it tells me that we must daily stay connected to God through prayer and bible study. Even the most studied theologian, prayer warrior and great evangelist, if you are not careful, you too can be deceived by the wiles of the devil.

Even with all of the predictions of future events, the bible makes it plain and clear that no one knows the time the Creator of the universe will return. There are many out there who have predicted and are still predicting that they can pin down when Jesus will return. The word of God is very clear on this. In verse 32 this is what Jesus says,

"But of that day and that hour knoweth no man, no, not the angels which are in heaven, neither the Son, but the Father".

Quit following groups and cults even if they are in your denomination or faith based organization. False prophets can be in your church or house, including the preacher. Ensure you are getting the word and not the presenter's opinion.

Our job is to stay on guard, stay on watch. Peter stated it best in his first epistle, I Peter 5:8, "Be sober, be vigilant; because your adversary the devil, as a roaring lion, walketh about, seeking whom he may devour," (KJV). We are to watch. We never know when the clouds will be rolled back as a scroll and the Son of Man will appear. Our prayer shall ever be that He does not come and find us sleeping.

REFLECTIONS ON MARK 14

BETRAYAL AND DENIAL

It is time for the Passover. The Pharisees, Scribes and Priests want to get rid of Jesus. However, they need an edge. They have tried trick after trick. Nothing has moved Him. The question ponders, how do we get Him? So, the plan, the plot falls right into their hands. Judas Iscariot, one of the twelve, one who has walked with Jesus for over 3 years makes a deal with the Chief Priests to betray Jesus. As the chapter says in verse 11, they even promised to give him money.

It is Passover time. Jesus sends the Disciples to secure a place. After securing a place and setting up, they were all seated and preparing for the meal when Jesus says in verse 18,

"...Verily I say unto you, One of you which eateth with me shall betray me", (KJV).

Now that was a shocker to them. They began to go one by one to ask the question, "Is it I?" It was one of the twelve. This is what Jesus said in verse 20,

"And He answered and said unto them, it is one of the twelve that dippeth with me in the dish", (KJV).

Have you ever been betrayed? Betrayal is never easy to accept; however, when it is someone that is not close to you, it is perceived in a different light. However, when it is someone that is close, it really stings and hurts. Judas was right there eating and participating in the Passover meal. They were dipping in the same bowl. Let's look at the definition of betrayal. According to the dictionary, it is the act of betraying or being disloyal to a person, group or group. In other words, to act in deliberate disloyalty. Betrayal destroys trust. Betrayal also sets out to mislead and or deceive.

Despite the upcoming betrayal by one of the twelve, He goes on with the Passover Supper. Jesus breaks bread and says in verse 22,

"Take it this is my body", (KJV). He then grabs the cup and verses 24 and 25 Jesus says, *"And He took the cup, and when He had given thanks, He gave it to them: and they all drank of it. And He said unto them, This is my blood of the new testament, which is shed for many. Verily I say unto you, I will drink no more of the fruit of the vine, until that day that I drink it new in the kingdom of God"*, (KJV).

Jesus is giving them a message. He is telling them this is the last meal we will enjoy together until we are together in the kingdom of God.

They were just not getting it. The betrayal by one of their own. Why is He saying that this bread at this Passover meal represents His body? What is He talking about not enjoying some good fruit juice until we drink it new in the kingdom of God? Now this is FRESH MANNA to them. But it doesn't stop there. Jesus now predicts Peter's betrayal. Verse 27 and 28 states,

"Then Jesus said to them, "All of you will be made to stumble because of Me this night, for it is written: I will strike the Shepherd, And The Sheep Will Be Scattered. But after I have been raised, I will go before you to Galilee", (KJV).

The bible is full of drama, plots and story lines. This is a main one. Peter, who was considered to be one Jesus' closes disciples, as well as James and John, is now being told by Jesus that he, Peter, will deny Him. Now Peter says even if all the rest of our friends run, I will not be one of them. It is interesting that we can be brave and jump to the challenge when the challenge is not in our presence at the time. Jesus even adds more fuel to the fire by telling him he will deny Him three times. Peter vehemently, as verse 30 puts it, denies that he would do that. He said that he would not deny Him but would die instead. Jesus had been warning them all the while, but they were not grasping the fact that He would suffer and die like a common criminal. It is easy to make a pledge, to volunteer to do something, however, when that time arrives and it's time to do the work or pay the pledge, we can't because we are now facing reality. Peter and his friends are making pledges that as this evening goes on, they will not keep. As I reflect on this and as we closer and closer to Jesus' death it is very obvious that the disciples after three plus years still have not grasped the concept of why Jesus came the first time. All they can see is Jesus getting them from under the iron feet of oppression placed on them by the Roman Empire. They had aspirations of being at the right and left hand of Jesus. They had aspirations of being senators and civil leaders in the new Jewish government. This night would not be the story ending that they had hoped and lived for.

Jesus knows the seriousness of this so He seeks a solace place where He can commune with His Father. He goes to a familiar setting, The Garden of Gethsemane. There He agonized with His Father. He said His soul was exceedingly sorrowful. In other words, Jesus was troubled and the weight of the sins of world was laying on His shoulders. Have you ever prayed for God to take something away from you? Maybe it was an illness or a financial burden, some family trouble. It weighs on you so heavy that you begin to plea for God to remove it. God does answer prayers and unfortunately if may not always be the answer we are seeking. Paul is a prime example when asked God to remove his physical ailment and God refused but responded by saying my grace is sufficient for you according to II Corinthians 12:7-9. But like Jesus we must recognize that our prayer request should always line up with the will of God. Mark records Jesus asking at least twice to have this cup, this burden passed from Him. However, Jesus finally in His prayer, in His plea says in verse 36, *"...nervetheless not what I will, but what thou wilt"*, (KJV). Is that our prayer request? No matter what we may ask, do we include telling God, not my will but your will be done? Let's face it, sometimes God's will may not be pleasant. His will may send us places we may not want to go, bring people in our lives we may not want to meet. His will may place us in circumstances that may shake our very foundation in our faith in Jesus. In Acts Chapter 16 God sent Paul to Macedonia. He was beaten and thrown in prison so he could save a jailer and his family. I believe it was God's will for Paul to go there. Paul attempted to go other places, but God blocked him and sent him to Macedonia because that was His will. God's will was for His Son, Jesus, to go through this suffering and ultimate death for us. Jesus, knowing what needed to be done in my mind actually won the battle in Gethsemane. Let me suggest to you that the battle is won on your knees in your prayer closet. I am a witness that is where the battle is won. During one of my valley experiences I was waiting to facilitate a Wednesday noon prayer service as I have done for the past six years. When I prayed for God to answer a particular prayer request, my prayer went from petition to praise. Before the day was over God answered my prayer with extra. In other words, not only did I get what I wanted, but I got extra. God will truly open the windows of heaven and pour you out a blessing and it may not always be cash money, but I promise it will be what you need.

As predicted, Jesus is betrayed by one of His own. Judas' signal was the one he kisses is the one to be arrested. So, he kissed Jesus and the Roman soldiers arrested Him. Jesus goes before the Sanhedrin. In our days, the church board. They accuse Him of blasphemy and condemned Him to die. The physical suffering now begins. Verse 65 of this chapter states,

> *"And some began to spit on him, and to cover His face, and to buffet Him, and to say unto Him, Prophesy: and the servants did strike Him with the palms of their hands"*, (KJV).

We have dealt with betrayal. Here is the denial. Peter, who stated He would never leave Jesus, said he would die for Jesus, now finds himself in position to face the music. Three times Peter denied Him. He even cursed and swore. Verse 71,

> *"But he began to curse and to swear, saying, I know not this man of whom ye speak"*, (KJV).

The one who said he would die for Christ is now denying that he even knows Jesus. Do we deny Christ as we travel down the corridors of life?

How do we live daily? Do we deny Him in how we treat one another? If we don't love Him, how can we love one another? Do you deny Him in your lifestyle? In everything we do, do we do it to the honor and glory of God? Do we live one life at church for 90 minutes and then take off the mask during the other times? I believe and live by I Samuel 2:30 which states, "… Be it far from me; for them that honor me I will honour," (KJV). Let's keep the faith and honor God with our lifestyle, how we treat others and with our generosity. God will honor your sincere efforts.

REFLECTIONS ON MARK 15

AND JUSTICE FOR ALL

The drama continues. After facing the Sanhedrin, which in our day, as mentioned, would be similar to a church board, and being both mentally and physically assaulted, He is taken to Pilate. Who was this Pilate? Pilate, whose full name was Marcus Pontius Pilate, was the Roman Governor of Judea.

Even though this was a legal court hearing I have called this debacle a "Kangaroo Court". Now the definition of Kangaroo Court, the part that raises eyebrows, is trying someone, especially without good evidence, as guilty of the crime or whatever the person is being accused of. As we have gone through the chapters of this gospel according to Mark, we have read how all through Jesus' ministry the religious leaders of that day were out to destroy Him. Now here is their opportunity. The devil was in the details.

Every Worship Experience when I welcome the congregation, I make this statement because it is true;

"ALL WEEK LONG THE DEVIL TRIED TO TAKE YOU OUT, BUT YOU
ARE HERE BECAUSE HE FAILED ONE MORE TIME"

The devil's goal is to take us out. We are God's prize possession of His creation and the devil hates us. Now he is doing everything he can to take Jesus out. And the plot thickens!

Charges are filed against Jesus and He never defended Himself. I am so intrigued at the fact that Jesus is now living in the will of His Father. While in His prayer closet wrestling with the wiles of the devil, He asked to have this burden, this cup to be taken from Him. However, He submitted to the will of God The Father. He is now in the "Kangaroo Court" setting and He says nothing to defend Himself. I have often asked the question, Why? Here is the answer, because despite the suffering He had already endured and the suffering He was presently going through, He was now in the will of God and He submitted totally to that will. Where are we when it comes to submitting to the will of God? Do we pray the prayer, thy will be done? Paul in Romans 8:34 repeats a verse that the Psalmist pens in Psalms 44:22, *"Yea, for thy sake are we killed all the day long; we are counted as sheep for the slaughter"*, (KJV). Paul also penned in II Timothy 3:12, *"Yea, and all that will live godly in Christ Jesus shall suffer persecution"*, (KJV). The world is hostile to God and His people. That's why Paul charges us in Romans 12:2 to not conform to this world, but to be transformed. If we are to be like Jesus, we must be transformed by the renewing of our mind.

It is amazing how one week we can be on top of world. We are making plenty of money, living in the best neighborhood, driving the best automobiles, traveling and just enjoying life. We are popular with everyone. Everyone wants to follow us and be with us. But when the bottom falls out you discover how many true friends and family you really have. Just a week before Jesus' dooming crucifixion, the crowd, "the church", had just thrown Him a parade and laid palm trees in His path as He rode through Jerusalem on a donkey. Now I am from New Orleans and we live and breathe Mardi Gras. Riding in on that donkey was equivalent to riding on a float as King of that particular Mardi Gras Club. This was huge. However, when the church leaders led a charge to destroy Him because He went against their man made "traditions", that same crowd is now shouting crucify Him!

There is a game called follow the leader. Let me suggest that you should be careful what leader you follow. Matthew 7:15 Jesus stated,

> *"Beware of false prophets, which come to you in sheep's clothing, but inwardly they are ravening wolves"*, (KJV).

Leaders whom have purposefully led people astray will be held accountable. Make sure that your leader is Christ led. Make sure that your leader is following, preaching, teaching and practicing the unadulterated word of God.

So, they work, the leaders, scribes, priests and Pharisees begin to stir up the crowd. There was a custom there, it's in the text, to release a prisoner for the Holiday Feast. Verse 6 – 8 says, *"Now at that feast he released unto them one prisoner, whomsoever they desired. And there was one named Barabbas, which lay bound with them that had made insurrection with him who had committed murder in the insurrection. And the multitude crying aloud began to desire him to do as he had ever done unto them"*, (KJV). Reflecting on this chapter just makes me think of all of the injustices in the world. Even today in 2020. Here in the land of the brave, the home of the free with liberty and justice for all. Daily people, especially minorities, in this country are wrongly accused and sentenced to long prison terms as well as sentenced to death even when they are innocent. I believe it was the intervention of God who caused the DNA test to come about as many innocent prisoners have been released from prison because of this test. Even after so-called witnesses pointed them out just because they fit a certain ethnic description.

Here in Jesus' case, He was innocent. He had not broken a law. Even Pilate recognized this, but He yielded to the will of the crowd who was incited by the leaders. Sound familiar? It is in the text, the yielding Pilate gives them a choice and chose a convicted murderer who they knew was guilty and shouted crucify Jesus. Life is all about choices. Our salvation is based on our choice. Whether we are saved is based on our choice. God does not force us to love, follow and be obedient to Him. He wants us to choose Him out of our own choice and free will. The crowd, the leaders, the church people chose the devil over Jesus. What a sad commentary of what transpired that day. Kangaroo Court found Him guilty of loving us with an everlasting love. Only true love would compel one to give up their life for a friend.

He was mocked, beaten, spit upon, teased, called a so-called king, given vinegar to drink and finally nailed to a cross with two other criminals who were guilty. What love that Jesus would give up His life even when many would not accept His gift or believe in Him. One of my favorite text in the bible is what Paul penned in Romans 5:8,

"But God commendeth His love toward us, in that, while we were yet sinners, Christ died for us", (KJV).

This is so powerful that Jesus would look down the corridors of time and see me messing up in all my unrighteousness and still died for me. This is so personal for me. My encouragement is that it becomes personal with you and you will accept His gift of giving up His life so that you and I would have the opportunity to live. It is truly "And Justice for All" if we accept His gift which will lead us to eternal life.

REFLECTIONS ON MARK 16

GO AND PREACH THE GOOD NEWS

The Gospel according to Mark ends with a beginning. How is that? The resurrection of Jesus, as I reflect on what Mark penned, was the beginning of a new era. Before the death of Christ, the sacrificial service of the sanctuary was the way to true forgiveness of our sins. It pointed to the actual sacrifice of the real Lamb of God.

When Jesus died the curtain in the temple was ripped from top to bottom. It opened the way for everyone to come boldly to the throne of grace. The Hebrew writer puts it this way:

> *"Seeing then that we have a great high priest, that is passed into the heavens, Jesus the Son of God; let us hold fast our profession. For we have an high priest which cannot be touched with the feeling of our infirmities; but was in all points tempted like as we are, yet without sin. Let therefore come boldly unto the throne of grace, that we may obtain mercy, and find grace to help in time of need,"* Hebrews 4:14-16, KJV.

Jesus' death and most importantly His resurrection, gives us this opportunity to come boldly! This is truly a new beginning. No longer do I have to go to a Priest, Bishop or Pastor. No longer do I have to bring a sacrificial spotless animal to shed blood. Jesus paid the price. However, had He not risen, there would-be no-good news.

The good news is that He has risen. The good news is He paid the price for your sins and mine. The good news is He conquered the grave. The good news is He has risen. So, what do we do with good news? We share good news. When you graduate from school, you share and tell everybody the good news of your accomplishments. When you get married you send out invitations inviting others to come to celebrate with you the occasion. When you have a child, you tell the world and have a party. When you get a promotion on your job, you are texting, emailing, "Instagramming" and tweeting to everyone the good news. Well, the gospel is the good news. What is that gospel? It is the saving power of Jesus Christ and it begins with:

> John 3:16, "For God so loved the world that He gave His only begotten son that whosoever believeth in Him, should not perish but have everlasting life", (KJV).

> I John 1:9, "If we confess our sins, He is faithful and just to forgive us our sins, and to cleanse us from all unrighteousness", (KJV).

> Romans 8:1, "There is therefore no condemnation to them which are in Christ Jesus, who walk not after the flesh but after the Spirit", (KJV).

> Romans 6:23, "For the wages of sin is death; but the gift of God is eternal life through Jesus Christ our Lord", (KJV).

The gospel, the good news is, He has risen and He has given us a commission. That commission is right here in our closing chapter of this book. Jesus after He has risen and meets with His team, He gives them their commission. It is right here in the text, Mark 16:15, "And He said unto them, Go ye into all the world, and preach the gospel to every creature", (KJV). What do you do with good news? You share it, you tell it, and you live it! It becomes an urgency and passion to ensure that everyone knows the good news.

Because He has risen, we are to preach, teach, baptize and teach and preach some more. We are to share and declare the goodness of our Lord and Savior Jesus Christ. Do not be discouraged by the issues and concerns of this world. Jesus will return! It is His promise and hold on to that blessed hope when He returns. Because when He returns there, He will proclaim the world of the "NO MORES". Revelation 21:4, John the Revelator speaks boldly proclaiming the world of the "NO MORES". Here is what John penned,

> *"And God shall wipe away all tears from their eyes; and there shall be no more death, sorrow, nor crying, neither shall there be any more pain: for the former things are passed away", (KJV).*

Let me paraphrase and make it personal. No more pain, no more heartache, no more diabetes, no more eye glasses, no more mortgage payments, no more disasters and disappointments, no more sadness and sorrow. I can go on and on as I reflect on the life, suffering, death, and resurrection of Jesus Christ.

These are the reflections of this humble servant on the gospel according to Mark. I ask that God bless you continually as you read these reflections and as you contemplate your own.

REFLECTIONS ON
THE BOOK OF LUKE

BE INSPIRED!

"*Many people have tried to tell the story of what God has done among us.*" Luke 1:1 CEV

Luke is determined to give an accurate account of what God did when Jesus walked the earth among us (Matthew 1:23). He reviewed and studied eyewitness accounts. He compared, scrutinized and recorded these accounts so that those of us who were not present at the time of Jesus's life could know the facts. What follows in this section of **Fresh Manna** are my reflections on what Luke shared in his Gospel. I am convinced that there is powerful, life altering inspiration buried in the Gospels. In each Gospel account, there is fresh manna for anyone willing to be open and teachable. By reflecting on Jesus, his life, ministry, death and resurrection, you come to know an awesome God who transforms, renews, empowers and equips us for life and eternal life.

The message from the angel given to Zechariah required his faith. He did not believe the word of the angel, (see vs. 20). No, Zechariah needed a sign. Are you ready to believe, to trust God's Word and His promises? As with Zechariah, God has plans for you. He is about to do something just for you. Do you believe Him? Can you trust Him? Will you trust Him? Even if what is promised seems impossible, unreasonable or absurd, God specializes in the impossible. *"Nothing is impossible with God!" Luke 1:37 CEV*

Amazingly, one month later, Mary received a message similar to Zechariah. While she had questions regarding the message, she did not disbelieve the word given to her. Because she did not fully understand what the angel Gabriel was saying to her, she reflected on those words, (see vs. 29). Reflecting is what we encourage you to do as we explore the Gospels. You will encounter passages that you may not understand. After reading this chapter, you may have more questions than answers. If this is true, that is okay. Reflect, ponder and think about what you are reading. Inspiration comes from outside of ourselves. It comes from the true Author of Scripture, see *2 Timothy 3:16, 17 NKJV*. There were many things which Jesus did throughout His life and ministry that Mary did not understand, (see *Luke 2:19, 51)*. Rather than leading her to doubt or disbelieve, the things she did not understand led her to contemplation and prayer. I believe when we reflect on scripture, the true Author of scripture gives insight and revelation not afforded to the casual reader. See *John 16:13-15*. Ponder, reflect and pray. Inspiration comes to those who believe.

REFLECTIONS FROM LUKE 2

OUR CHILDREN MATTER

Jesus became wise, and he grew strong. God was pleased with him and so were the people. Luke 2:52 CEV

Children do not become wise, strong and pleasing to God and people by accident. Faithful, loving, nurturing and praying parents or guardians cultivate these characteristics. Child rearing is challenging. Luke chapters 1 and 2 reveal that the parents of John as well as the parents of Jesus contributed to their children's successes. Both mothers, Elizabeth and Mary, recognized their son as a gift from God. They understood that God had a plan and purpose for their lives. They submitted to Gods' plan for rearing their child. Elizabeth had the support and example of Zechariah and Mary had the support and example of Joseph. These parents understood that diet, social exposure, education, spiritual connection and physical development were each critical contributors in rearing their child to fulfill the purpose they were born to achieve. Being a good parent requires faith. One must be obedient to God in all matters related to their child. Being a good parent requires hard work, consistent practices and passionate prayer. Many situations might cause one to think there is no hope for today's children and youth. When you consider the drug epidemic, gang recruitment, peer pressure, access to explicit materials, exposure to racist propaganda, the magnetic pull of the internet, the mesmerizing hold of music and the constant blast of negativity through media, it is very easy to think that there is no hope. These things among others cast our children and youth into the depths of depression and doubt, often leading them to various disorders, even suicidal and hopeless thoughts.

Yet there is hope for our children. The hope of which I speak starts with us. Whether you are a new parent or your children have children of their own, it is never too late to be a parent like those who raised John and Jesus. Today is the time to begin being a faithful, praying parent. Everything you do for and with your children matters. From naming your child to recognizing that your child is never too young to learn, or never too old to teach, to faithfully taking them to church, to worshiping with them at home. Everything you do for and with your children matters. Love your children the way God loves. Reflect on your child's interest. Do your best to understand how God may use their unique gift for His glory.

Recently, my oldest son called to say thank you for allowing him and his group of friends to Rap in church when they were young. Many people told him in those days that Rap music had no place in the church and that it was of the devil. It was not God's music. However, I encouraged him to write and present his craft. I believed his creativity, his writing skills and his ability to communicate in this way was his gift from God. Today my son is an award winning music artist. He has had Top 10 songs and been honored for his musical lyrics. My son is also a minister now. He is a phenomenal preacher and one of my favorite speakers. His messages are like his music; creative, relevant and powerfully, positively influencing people leading them to new life. He is confident he is who he is today because his parents supported his gifts.

Our children will become wise and strong. They will be pleasing to God and to people when we remain faithful to our calling as parents. It is when we prepare, equip, pray for and make ready our children for service that they become what God intends.

REFLECTIONS FROM LUKE 3

THE SKILL OF UN-COMFORTABILITY

"At that time God spoke to Zechariah's son John, who was living in the desert. ³So John went along the Jordan Valley, telling the people, "Turn back to God and be baptized! Then your sins will be forgiven." Luke 3:2, 3 CEV

There are three meaningful discoveries I find upon reflection of chapter 3.

First, John was faithful to his purpose even though what he was doing, and where he was doing it was unpopular. John was in the desert or wilderness. He was in an uncomfortable place. The desert, hot, humid, and desolate is a tough place to do ministry. People do not congregate in the desert. It was not the popular meeting spot. The desert was not the place to go to find large crowds. It was not one of the prevalent populated places of the day. Yet it was here, in the desert that John set up his pulpit and platform to proclaim a message of repentance.

Not only was John in an uncomfortable place, he was also proclaiming a message that would disturb the comfort of his listeners. His was a message of repentance. Typically, people flock to listen to messages that are easy to hear. While these type of sermons are inclined and even designed to produce shouts of praise they rarely lead to a change of the heart. These comfortable, easy to hear messages tend to be popular. They contribute to good feelings but seldom bring conviction that lead to a transformed life. People tend to gravitate toward such preachers. Paul in his letter to Timothy addresses this.

²Preach the word. Be ready to do it whether it is convenient or inconvenient. Correct, confront, and encourage with patience and instruction. ³There will come a time when people will not tolerate sound teaching. They will collect teachers who say what they want to hear because they are self-centered. ⁴They will turn their back on the truth and turn to myths. 2 Timothy 4:2-4 CEB

This leads to my second discovery in Luke 3. Good preaching convicts. John was bold and courageous in his preaching. He called for people to change.

He admonished them to live a better life in every way (*verses 3-14*). He was no respecter of persons. He preached repentance to everyone including the religious, political and civic leaders of the day. Those who heard John's preaching asked, "What should we do?" (Verse 10). Reading the Word or hearing the Word will produce transformation. John's preaching made it clear that hearing the word does not only cause one to rejoice, but it should lead one to change. Where there is dishonesty, it leads to integrity. Where there is ugliness, it leads to kindness. Where there is hatred it, leads to love. The change is so significant that it may lead to baptism. Baptism symbolizes a death to the old self and a resurrection of a new you (See Romans 6:3, 4). When you read the Bible, or listen to a sermon, does it convict you? Do you examine yourself to determine if you practice what you have read or heard? John, like James encourages us to be doers of the word and not just hearers (See James 1:22).

The third discovery from Luke 3 is family connections matter.

"... The family of Jesus went all the way back to Adam and then to God." vs. 38

In Bible reading, I have often skipped over the long list of hard to pronounce and awkwardly spelled names, like the list in verses 23-38. However, it is worth our time to reflect on this lineage. Have you reviewed your family history and connections? It could be when you review it you will discover answers that could clear up questions that have stifled you. Generational connections have proven helpful in the medical realm. Your family health history may help to understand your own health challenges. Generational connections can help identify and explain some habits and/or behaviors. It might speak to why you lean toward a certain profession or hobby over another. It may also help one to understand why some challenges in life are harder to overcome. Looking back should never be our primary focus. Nevertheless, looking back to understand may allow us to tap into a powerful understanding that will propel us forward. Reviewing one's family history is not for the purpose of judging or condemning yourself or others. Review your family history to gain a deeper understanding of who you are, and where you come from. You have a history. If you trace it fully you will discover that you come from God. Anyone with that history can have an amazing future.

REFLECTIONS FROM LUKE 4

KEEP ON

Luke 4:44 - "So He kept on preaching..." When you have a reason for existing, when there is a calling on your life, when it is clear God desires to employ you in His service, you will be tested and challenged to quit. In an attempt to convince you to give up and stop you could encounter threats. All this Jesus endured in Luke 4, but He did not stop. Luke proclaims, "He kept on preaching!"

What is it that God has called you to do? Whatever it is, keep doing it. Keep on when ridiculed! Keep on when reminded of your past! You may be fearful of mistakes, but keep on! Because God has called you, keep on! Be empowered by the same Spirit of God that propelled Jesus. KEEP ON!

Test and challenges could be obstacles used to trip you up. An important key to keeping on and not stumbling is to know the Word of God. In every instance where Jesus was tested, He leaned on and relied on the Word of God (see vs. *34, 8, 10*). It is imperative to note that the Power is not in you. The power is in God and in His Word. The encouragement is not to be strong in your own strength, but in God's strength (See *Ephesians 6:10*).

Remember this, being in challenging and testing situations is not necessarily proof you have done something wrong or that you are outside of God's will. God may lead you into tough times to prepare you for your purpose. Trust that God is leading even when led into a test. Do not crack under pressure. Do not forget your purpose when you are under pressure. Not everyone will respond favorably to your purpose, but stay true to it. Staying true will fulfill you and bless others. Be confident of your purpose. Take deliberate steps to fulfill your purpose. Do not worry about making mistakes. The One who called you is with you. He has covered you in every way.

Some of the ones who were trying to stop Jesus in chapter 4 were good people. They were the very ones blessed by His preaching and teaching.

The next morning Jesus went out to a place where he could be alone, and crowds came looking for him. When they found him, they tried to stop him from leaving. However, Jesus said, "People in other towns must hear the good news about God's kingdom. This is why I was sent," Luke 4:42, 43.

The very ones whom you are blessing with your preaching and teaching can become instruments used to derail you from your purpose.

Recognize that Jesus was intentional about spending time alone with God. To handle the pressure that comes to servants of God, it is essential to spend time alone with God. Alone time with God refreshes you and rekindles your calling and your purpose. When good intentioned people tried to stop Jesus, He reminded them of why He came. Never forget your purpose. Remember your why. Remember your calling. Keep on and do not stop.

REFLECTIONS FROM LUKE 5

ATTRACTED TO YOU EVEN MORE

**"When Simon Peter saw this happen, he knelt down in front of Jesus and said, "Lord, don't come near me! I am a sinner.""
Luke 5:8 CEV**

Our mistakes, or problems and our sinfulness repel most people, but not God. He is attracted to us even more when we acknowledge we are sinful and allow Him to move into our lives. When Jesus began His search for disciples to train and prepare for leadership he did not go to the synagogues or the schools of the prophets. He found people whose fitness for service was questionable. To name a few, there was impetuous Peter, whose language was at times vulgar to say the least, and his brother Andrew. There were the sons of thunder, James and John (see *Mark 3:17*), also Matthew, a tax collector. Most tax collectors, also known as publicans, had a reputation for being dishonest and regularly charged tax payers more than what they owed (see *Luke 3:12, 13*). Those chosen by Jesus were not righteous, nor were they perfect. Those messed up; those broken, those lost, and the sinful are the ones selected.

It is amazing that these are the very ones God is looking for. They are the ones He came to save.

Verses 31-32 "Jesus answered, "Healthy people don't need a doctor, but sick people do. I didn't come to invite good people to turn to God. I came to invite sinners."

The reason Jesus is not repelled by our sins is two-fold. One, He loves us. Whether dirty, broken or rejected by everyone else, He loves us. Second, He is able to forgive us of our sins.

In verse 20 He says, "Your sins are forgiven!"

The religious people near by took issue with this statement, however, Jesus confirms He has the right and the power to forgive our sins. Regardless of what others may think, you are most certainly forgiven when Jesus forgives you!

If you have sin, if you have issues, if you have problems, you are the one Jesus is calling to be His disciple. He is not repulsed by your condition. He is the Great Physician who is able to heal you. As we say in New Orleans, Believe Dat!

"But Jesus would often go to some place where he could be alone and pray, Luke 5:16

Sinners make the best disciples. Recognize and acknowledge that you are a sinner. Allow Jesus to touch you the way he touched the leper, (see *vs. 13*). Allow Jesus to forgive you the way He forgave the man who could not walk, (see *vs. 20, 24-26*) Jesus has power to heal, to forgive and to save. Be His great miracle today!

REFLECTIONS FROM LUKE 6

ALL EYES ON YOU

"Some Pharisees and teachers of the Law of Moses kept watching Jesus to see if he would heal the man. They did this because they wanted to accuse Jesus of doing something wrong. Luke 6:7 CEV

Jesus was constantly being watched, observed, and scrutinized. Some, especially the religious leaders, carefully watched him, not to be able to copy him or mimic his actions but observed to criticize him. They watched him so that they could catch Him in some wrongdoing.

If this was true for Jesus, do not be surprised when it happens to you. You will have critics who will focus on your flaws and proclaim them fatal. They will trace your steps and count every misstep. They will scrutinize every word you speak and twist what you say until they have woven a lie. Whenever you seek to do good there will be accusers who will pounce on your bad. Whenever you attempt to build, there will be accusers who will work to tear down what you have built. Accusation is a powerful weapon. The enemy of our souls has used it since his time in heaven, (see *Revelations 12:9-11*). However, Jesus took care of the accuser then and will take care of accusers today. As in chapter *5* Jesus consistently handled this, and any kind of attack with the Sword, (see *Ephesians 6:17*) or in other words, by referring to scripture, (see *vs. 3, 4*). The sword defends and attacks. One is not passive when wheeling a sword.

He also took care of Himself by spending time alone in prayer, (see *vs. 12*). Do not take lightly the reading of scripture and private time in prayer. Being faithful to these disciplines will not only lead to greater positive change and blessing but will give you the authority to deal with the accusers you will encounter in your walk with God.

Daily Bible study along with a faithful and consistent prayer life will:

- Bless and grow you through adversity, (*vs. 20-24*).

- Empower you to treat people well regardless of how they treat you (*vs. 37, 38*).

- Teach you to examine yourself, and in doing so, planting yourself on a solid foundation and producing good fruit (*vs. 39-49*).

All eyes will be on you. Some are only watching to find an opportunity or reason to criticize. Others are watching because they are simply curious. Still some watch because they believe something miraculous will happen. Regardless of the reason you will be watched, give your spectators something to see. Allow them to see something special. Let them to see that God is at work in your life. When He is at work powerful things happen and those powerful and amazing things will be seen, (see Matthew 5:16).

JUST HOW MUCH DO YOU LOVE ME

"When these messengers came to Jesus, they said, "John the Baptist sent us to ask, Are you the one we should be looking for? Or are we supposed to wait for someone else?" At that time Jesus was healing many people who were sick or in pain or were troubled by evil spirits, and he was giving sight to a lot of blind people. Jesus said to the messengers sent by John, "Go and tell John what you have seen and heard. Blind people are now able to see, and the lame can walk. People who have leprosy are being healed, and the deaf can now hear. The dead are raised to life, and the poor are hearing the good news. God will bless everyone who doesn't reject me because of what I do." Luke 7:20-23 CEV

The recognition and acknowledgement of who Jesus is brings Forgiveness, Hope, Healing and Salvation.

The army officer's servant healed, the widows son brought back to life, John the one who baptizes, encouraged by the ministry and miracles Jesus performed, the woman who washed Jesus's feet with her tears, forgiven. Each one of these precious people recognized and acknowledged Jesus for who He was. The recognition and acknowledgements they gave produced tremendous blessings in each of their lives. This recognition and acknowledgement confirmed who they were and who He is. They made it clear that they knew the difference.

Ponder this question. Do you believe you are forgiven? I love the ending of this chapter. The woman at Simon's party never stopped kissing Jesus' feet. Jesus had done so much for her that her gratitude was unending. Simon, who more than anyone should have had a similar response when welcoming Jesus, was critical of the woman. He knew her past. He would not have forgiven a past like hers, and believed neither should anyone else. Some people will criticize you. They may remind you of who you were or what you have done in your past. Do not allow these ungrateful agents of the enemy, accusers of the saints, to stifle your actions or mute your praise. Instead, listen to Jesus,

"But Jesus told the woman, "Because of your faith, you are now saved. May God give you peace!" Luke 7:50 CEV

REFLECTIONS FROM LUKE 8

A WOMAN'S WORK

"Soon after this, Jesus was going through towns and villages, telling the good news about God's kingdom. His twelve apostles were with him, and so were some women who had been healed of evil spirits and all sorts of diseases. One of the women was Mary Magdalene, who once had seven demons in her.

There is always talk of the 12 apostles of Jesus, however, in Luke 8, scripture reveals that Jesus had disciples who were women. It is interesting to note that these female disciples were instrumental in helping to finance the ministry of Jesus. Some of these women experienced healing from Him and others delivered from demon possession. Not every person healed in this way was invited to stay among the direct followers of Jesus, (see *vs. 38, 39*) but Mary Magdalene was. Some women were influential, like Joanna who was married to an official in King Herod's court. Women, like men were an important part of Jesus' ministry and ministerial success.

An eastern, male dominated culture served as the backdrop for the written Word. In this culture, women found themselves marginalized, taken for granted, ignored or forgotten. How exciting to know that this was not so with Jesus. Women were not only included but also essential and important to the work He performed.

Women, in society and in the church, offer gifts and bring skills to the table that Jesus recognized. So should we! Women give perspectives men often fail to consider. Women speak to certain issues men struggle to address. Women are generous and influential. Women are a necessary and essential part of sharing the Gospel.

Today some struggle with women in leadership, women earning more than men, women preaching, and more. Luke 8 points out the fact that women have a place in God's work, in the church and in society as a whole.

If a woman or a man's heart is good soil, the spiritual seed planted will take root and grow. In the same way, if the soil has issues the seed will suffer and not grow, (*vs. 4-15*). If a woman or a man has gifts why hide it, (*vs. 16-18*)? If a storm listens to and obeys Jesus, should not we listen and obey when it comes to women in His service, (*vs. 22-25*)?

Luke 8 calls for an awakening in our understanding that in Christ all are ONE, (see Galatians 3:28)! Male, female, black, white, US citizen, immigrant, all are one in Jesus.

REFLECTIONS FROM LUKE 9

SHARE, SERVE, SACRIFICE

"Jesus answered, "You give them something to eat." But they replied, "We have only five small loaves of bread and two fish. If we are going to feed all these people, we will have to go and buy food."" **Luke 9:13 CEV**

Jesus appears to be preparing his followers to do the following: share, serve and sacrifice. He is aware that the time is fast approaching when He will no longer be with them. As a result, He equips his disciples with power to teach and heal, (*vs. 1, 2, and 6*). Part of His plan for them is that they share their gifts and share the good news they have experienced with others.

When the disciples looked out on the vast crowd of people who came to hear Jesus' teachings, they recognized their need for nourishment. They demonstrated a compassion they learned from Jesus Himself. However, their initial thought was to send the crowd away so that they could address this need themselves. They saw the concern as the crowd's problem. The crowd needed to find the solution. They needed to fix this issue themselves. Yet Jesus had a different reaction to the crowd's need. Jesus said to the disciples "you meet their need!" He then demonstrated how to do so. Jesus served a meal to 5,000 men with a boy's small lunch.

Many see the glory of a life with Christ and desire that glory alone (see *vs. 28-36 & 46-48*), but to be a true disciple requires sacrifice, (*vs. 22-27, & 57-62*). To share, serve and sacrifice requires full faith and faithfulness to ones beliefs as well as quality time alone with God. Time alone with God increases one's confidence in God and in His Word. Herod was worried and troubled because he was unsure of his beliefs (*vs. 7-9*). The more we spend time with God and His Word the greater our surety. Unlike Herod, we will know that we know that we know, and not have doubt or confusion when presented with situations that challenge our faith.

A lack of faith can render us powerless in critical moments. The disciples failed to heal a very sick boy because they lacked faith (*vs. 40, 41*). Alone time with God will help to grow the kind of faith that gives us power (see *Hebrews 11*).

Jesus modeled how time alone in prayer is the key to being a successful disciple (*vs. 10, 18, 28*). It is important for us to spend quality alone time with God or like the Disciples of Christ; we will experience more failure in life than necessary. Success can be ours as we listen to and follow the example of Jesus.

REFLECTIONS FROM LUKE 10

DO, DO, DO, WHAT A MESS

"The Lord answered, "Martha, Martha! You are worried and upset about so many things, but only one thing is necessary. Mary has chosen what is best, and it will not be taken away from her."" Luke 10:41, 42 CEV

We experience personal growth and positive change, not because of the work we do, but because of the time spent with the Change Agent, Jesus. Martha was busy working; however, Mary was busy growing and changing by because she stayed engaged with Jesus. Mary, according to Jesus, made the best decision.

Our work, careers, professions, jobs, are important. The work we do in the church, our missionary work, community service efforts and our volunteer service participation are all noble, important and meaningful. The time we spend doing these things blesses others, elevates life and helps to meet our needs providing the resources necessary to do well in life. Accolades and honor often come because of our work contributions. The affirmations we receive because of our labor compels us to work harder, push longer and do more. As we excel in our professions, often the rewarded is promotions, titles, offices, opportunities, and increased income. This causes us to work even more and do and do and do. My friend Jeff Flowers says, "We do so much until we do do on everything!" What a mess! Doing becomes a mess when work becomes our priority. Prioritizing work rather than relationships causes us to miss transformational connections. In *Matthew 7:21-23* there is revealed a collection of workers who were so busy working that they never took time to know the one they were working for. Jesus proclaims to them that despite all the accolades they trumpet, "*I never knew you*". Their working resume was strong, but their relational connection was weak. In reality, it was nonexistent.

Time with Jesus is essential and necessary. Time spent with Him equips us for our work. Time with Jesus is the key to success in work and in ministry. This is our power source when introducing others to Jesus, (*vs. 1-17*). Time with Jesus establishes a solid divine connection. Time with Jesus is the key to knowing God for ourselves, (*vs. 21-24*). Time with Jesus enhances earthly relationships. This is the key to caring, respectful relationships with others, (*vs. 25-37*). When you choose to spend time with God daily, you are choosing as Jesus said, "that which is best!" By staying faithful to this daily commitment, you will come to know God better and you will know Him for yourself. It is in knowing God that you become more aware of your own shortcomings and needs. Knowing Him creates a desire to do better and be better. Knowing Him is what changes lives! As important as our work may be, it does not supersede, override or cancel out our greatest need. That is, the need to do as Mary did. Choose the best! Spending time relationally with God.

REFLECTIONS FROM LUKE 11

I CAN BE TAUGHT

"When Jesus had finished praying, one of his disciples said to him, Lord, teach us to pray, just as John taught his followers to pray." Luke 11:1 CEV

Jesus' prayer life was faithful, regular and consistent. The disciples were aware that Jesus possessed amazing power. They were also aware that this power was available to Him because of His prayer connection with His Father. Even though the disciples were aware of this, they were unsure how to pray in the way that Jesus prayed. Therefore, they made a special request.

They did not ask to learn how to heal the sick. They did not ask how to walk on water. They did not ask how to raise the dead. No, what they asked for was the key to any believer's power. For instruction on how to pray was their request. Jesus' disciples were aware that John taught his followers the power of prayer. They were witnesses to the impact and power prayer produced in Jesus' daily experience. They wanted the same power Jesus demonstrated when confronted with an array of challenging people and intensely troubling situations. They were eager and ready to learn how to pray.

Jesus then teaches them what we've come to know as the Lord's Prayer, *(vs. 2-4)*. He teaches them to be persistent and faithful in prayer, *(vs. 5-14)*. He reminds them that prayer keeps our spiritual house occupied with God's Spirit, preventing evil from ruling and ruining our lives, *(vs. 24-26)*. He makes clear that prayer gives us boldness much in the same way it gave Jesus the boldness to speak truth and to speak rebuke when needed, *(vs. 37-54)*.

Most people, even "religious" people have an easy time speaking rebuke but a difficult time receiving it. Jesus' admonition and correction is given to religious people, especially to leadership. Their reaction to His correction is not self-reflection or self-evaluation. No, their unfortunate and sad reaction was to figure out the best way to get even with the one giving the rebuke. "How can we get even with Jesus?" *(vs. 53)*. Most people do not want correction. Some children despise the rebuke of parents. Husbands or wives despise the rebuke of their spouse. Students despise the rebuke of teachers. There are employees who despise the rebuke of their supervisor. Rather than prayerfully reflect on the correction given, some prefer to "get even". Some retaliate with no consideration that the correction is in their best interest. Pray before you correct someone. In the same way, when corrected pray. There are times when we need to speak to those who have stepped out of bounds. There are times when we need speaking to because we have stepped out of bounds. Be mindful that all these times require prayer.

Are you prayerful about everything? Do you pray about the criticism you receive? Do you ask for insight and understanding when criticized? Do you become defensive immediately? Are you thankful for correction? Do you accept criticism and correction with gratitude? On the other hand, are you that person who attempts to point out the wrongs of the person who brings criticism to you? Do you try to get even? Know this, in all situations, with all people, at all times, PRAY! This is where your power will come from.

REFLECTIONS FROM LUKE 12

I AM SO PROUD OF YOU

"If you tell others that you belong to me, the Son of Man will tell God's angels that you are my followers." Luke 12:8 CEV

God values us more than we realize, (*vs. 7*). The more we come to know Him, the more willing we will be to share who He is in our lives and what He has done for us.

God, like a proud parent, brags on us.

"Have you considered my servant Job?" Job 1:8. "David, a man after my own heart." Acts 13:22.

Although flawed, sinful or broken, God claims us as His own without reservation or hesitation. We are the *"apple of His eye"* (*Psalm 17:8*). We are His pearls of great price, (*Matthew 13:45, 46*). His concern for even the smallest of creatures illustrates His heart for us, (*vs 6*). His concern for us is beyond comprehension. He is so thoughtful about us that he even knows the number of every hair on our heads (*vs.7*). He values us so much that when our fore-parents, Adam and Eve sinned, He put in motion a plan already outlined to redeem us, to reclaim us, and to save us. That plan required the greatest sacrifice that anyone could make. It required the death of Jesus, His only begotten Son, (*John 3:16*). That demonstration of love is the greatest display of the value God places in us.

Are you just as honored, proud and willing to talk about God, as He is to talk about you? Are you willing to share with others all that He has done and is doing in your life? *Luke 12* reminds us why it is easy to talk about this amazing God. For starters, we live in a world that is full of worry and anxiety. There are concerns about jobs, health care and the retirement years. There is anxiety about homelessness, infant mortality, drug abuse, crime, debt, disease, war, global warming and so much more. In the midst of all that concern people, God says, "Worry not! I've got you." He says when you seek my righteousness and me; all these things will be added to you, (*vs. 31*). Knowing God keeps us worry free. Knowing that He supplies all our needs, gives us a testimony worth sharing. Knowing that He is thinking about our wellbeing in this life, and that beyond this life He is laying up treasures just for us, gives us something to talk about (*vs. 32-34*). It also gives us a reason to be faithful servants, (*vs. 35-48*).

God is not ashamed of us. Even in a tattered broken, sinful condition, He looks upon us proudly and proclaims, "That one is mine!" With Him, we have nothing to be ashamed. Let us not be ashamed of Him. It is our honor to share with boldness, what He is doing for us. Have you read *Acts 29*? Some would tell you it does not exist, that there are only 28 chapters in the book of Acts. *Acts 1-28* are the Acts of the Apostles. *Acts 29* is the gospel according to you. It is your story. It is about your relationship with God. Do not be ashamed to share that story.

REFLECTIONS FROM LUKE 13

JUST A LITTLE MORE TIME PLEASE

"Jesus then told them this story: A man had a fig tree growing in his vineyard. One day he went out to pick some figs, but he didn't find any. The gardener answered, "Master, leave it for another year. I'll dig around it and put some manure on it to make it grow. Maybe it will have figs on it next year. If it doesn't, you can have it cut down.""

God is gracious to us. He is long suffering with us. His desire is not to lose any of us, but ultimately the choice is ours to stay in His grace or to remove ourselves from His grace. *Luke 13:6-9* presents a request for an unproductive fig tree. The request is to give the unfruitful, unproductive tree more time to produce, more time to be productive. The request for additional time is honored, however, at some point time runs out and the tree is cut down. *Luke 13* is a reminder to us of God's grace and His goodness. It is important not to take God's grace lightly. God is willing to give extensions but He does expect production. If planted in Him, we will produce fruit that displays our connection to Him. If we do not produce fruit, it is an indication that we are not connected. To have life one must be and remain connected to the source of life, (see John 15:1-6).

While God is gracious and gives extensions, it is important to be mindful that we live in a sinful world. With sin came death. People die daily. Some die in the worse ways. Their death is not an indication that they are terrible sinners. Jesus points this out in *vs. 1-5* and admonishes us to turn to God while we have the opportunity.

> *Hebrews 3:15* reminds us, *"Today if you will hear His voice, do not harden your heart" NKJV.*

Postponing a decision for God may be a fatal mistake. This is not because God is unwilling to embrace us but that at some point the clock hits triple zeros and the buzzer sounds. At that time, time is up.

On January 26, 2020, basketball great Kobe Bryant, along with his 13 year old daughter Gianna and seven others died in a helicopter crash. Kobe, after attending a church service, began traveling via helicopter with the group to a youth basketball tournament. Who knew this would be his last flight. Who knew that for him there would be no opportunities later for hugs, well wishes, dinner, games, or any other meaningful life exchanges? James 4:14 makes this crystal clear.

> *"What do you know about tomorrow? How can you be so sure about your life? It is nothing more than mist that appears for only a little while before it disappears."*

Often people ask, "Won't God accept me even if it's last minute?" There are examples of this very thing in scripture. We find one such example shared later in *Luke 23:42.* The thief on the cross, in his last moments of life he asked to be remembered and was promised by the Savior that he would be remembered. God does not want to lose any of us. His desire is that none perishes, (see 2 Peter 3:9). Know this, God has the ability to take your barren life and make it fruitful throughout all your days. He wants us to be productive and fruitful. Last minute request for salvation is not only risky, but prevents lifelong positive production and fruitfulness. Jesus illustrates what a life with Him can be like, how it is changed, enhanced and made more wonderful. He does so when he encounters a woman who for 18 years suffered a bent over condition and could in no way fix herself (*vs. 10-17*). After connecting with Jesus, not only did her life straighten out, but her physical appearance as well. She stood tall. She told her story to the glory to God. Life with God produces wonderful change that will make you better and productive. One of the products of being better is the ability to rejoice.

Waiting to make a decision for God only delays your change and your testimony. It does not take a titanic, gigantic, occurrence to have a fruit producing experience with God. The smallest experience with God produces phenomenal results, (vs. 16-20).

There are no limits for Jesus. He will go to any extreme to save you. "Jerusalem, Jerusalem! Your people have killed the prophets and have stoned the messengers who were sent to you. I have often wanted to gather your people, as a hen gathers her chicks under her wings. But you wouldn't let me" *Luke 13:34 CEV*. Think about this, if you are reading this book *Fresh Manna*, God is still with you. Because you are still living, there is still hope. Make a decision right now to be a fruit-producing child of God. Decide now to embrace the forgiveness extended to you, to be accepted and to allow God to empower you to be productive and fruitful. This is that narrow way into the kingdom. This is the way to eternal life with Him, (vs. 22-30).

REFLECTIONS FROM LUKE 14

STILL PRODUCTIVE

"Salt is good, but if it no longer tastes like salt, how can it be made to taste salty again? It is no longer good for the soil or even for the manure pile. People simply throw it out. If you have ears, pay attention!" Luke 14:34, 35 CEV

It is critically important for us to maintain our spiritual connection with God. It is imperative to keep fresh this connection because it affects our effectiveness. Losing effectiveness comes at a great cost. We cannot afford to lose our effectiveness. Losing effectiveness is like salt that has lost its flavor. The salt is good for nothing. When we lose effectiveness, it negatively affects our lives in multiple ways. It influences our judgment, especially when interpreting and applying God's Word, (vs. 1-6). Interpreting and applying God's Word requires godly wisdom and a clear ability to make good judgements. People who have lost their effectiveness tend to use

God's Word for many self-serving reasons. To promote slavery, to devalue women, and to procure personal wealth are just a few ways people who have lost their connection to God have misapplied His Word.

Losing effectiveness negatively affects relational & social decisions, (*vs. 8-14*). Growing up in New Orleans I was very aware of the nuances that made the Crescent City unique. I was comfortable with the customs and practices I learned growing up in my hometown. When I transitioned to Texas for college, I learned quickly there is a much larger world and that people from varied places do things differently. They relate differently. They enjoy different foods and music. My true awakening came when I realized what they did and the way they did it was not wrong, just different. It was tasteless and insensitive for me to expect that everyone would negotiate life and operate the exact way people in New Orleans do. Being understanding of cultural, ethnic, religious and other differences allows me to establish stronger connections with others that help me maintain my effectiveness, relationally and socially.

Losing effectiveness can negatively affect financial decisions, (*vs. 28-30*). The feeling that one has wasted hard-earned money is a most horrible feeling. Please understand that a connection with God does not provide spiritual blessings alone. God blesses our increase, our income, our ability to earn and save so that we are financially secure. A lack of effectiveness can lead to squandering resources, compulsive spending habits, and other practices that will negatively affect our finances. Little becomes much when we maintain our effectiveness. We see our resources multiply and our blessings increase when we stay connected to God.

We must maintain our connection with God. This is what leads us to a deeper loving relationship with Him. This is the key to true discipleship, (*vs. 25-27*).

REFLECTIONS FROM LUKE 15

EVERY ONE OF US

"Tax collectors and sinners were all crowding around to listen to Jesus. So the Pharisees and the teachers of the Law of Moses started grumbling, This man is friendly with sinners. He even eats with them." Luke 15:1, 2 CEV

Luke 15 reveals 3 types of people. Can you identify yourself in this chapter? Being able to recognize who you are is a major step to discovering a Savior who desires to be your friend.

The first group found in *Luke 15* are those who are sinners. They are lost, separated and need support, love, compassion and a Savior. This group includes everyone without exception or exclusion, whether we believe this or not. Some people know they are lost and cannot find their way back, as in the parable of the lost sheep, *vs. 3-7*. Others are lost and have no clue that they are lost, as in the parable of the lost coin, *vs. 8-10*. Still others decide to separate themselves from the Father. They make multiple bad choices which leaves them broken, destitute and with the knowledge that they have messed up in a huge way, *vs. 11-24*. All are lost. All are in need of a Savior, (see *Romans 3:23*).

The next group revealed are those who express their displeasure that the lost are embraced, welcomed, accepted and celebrated, *vs. 2, 25-32*. Be reminded that this angry, bitter complaining group of people are a part of the first group mentioned. They too are sinners. They are most likely a lost coin. They are lost and do not know it. Maybe they were lost, then found, but forgot that this was their experience. It is amazing how quickly some forget that they too needed saving from something. People at times forget the thing from which God saved them. Whatever the case, this group of people cannot find the heart to celebrate what God can do or is doing in the lives of people who clearly need the love and forgiveness of a Savior. This group of people are judgmental, unforgiving, and have long memories, even keeping records of wrongs committed. This group is bitter rather than better. They are selfish rather than sacrificing. They are forgetful rather than forgiving.

The final group revealed are those who celebrate and rejoice when someone who has been lost is found, *vs. 6, 9, 10, 22-24, 32*. God rejoices. The angels in heaven celebrate. Any and all who have experienced God's love, grace and forgiveness will celebrate as well.

Jesus came to find and reclaim those who are lost. When He finds the lost, He celebrates in an open and demonstrative way. He then admonishes us to, in the words of Kool & the Gang's 1980s hit, "celebrate good times, come on!"

It is clear and it is a fact that everyone is in the first group revealed in Luke 15. We are all sinners. The hope is that we all will avoid the second group altogether and be a meaningful part of this third group. This group consist of those who become thrilled, ecstatic and excited. They cannot stop celebrating or rejoicing because the once lost are now found!

REFLECTIONS FROM LUKE 16

WHERE IS YOUR HEART?

**"*The Pharisees really loved money. So when they heard what Jesus said, they made fun of him. But Jesus told them: You are always making yourselves look good, but God sees what is in your heart. The things that most people think are important are worthless as far as God is concerned" Luke 16:14, 15*

Your heart is what really matters. Where is your heart? Clothes, accessories, houses, cars, decorations, things and stuff all make us look good. Externally, they give the look of success. However, your heart determines if you are truly successful.

Wealth in this life is not an indication that God has blessed or accepted you no more than not have much worldly goods is an indication that you are outside of God's will. Jesus tells the story of the Rich man and Lazarus to illustrate this hard for some to believe concept, *vs. 19-31*.

Regardless of how little or how much we have, faithfulness with it is the admonition.

"Those who can be trusted in little matters can also be trusted with important matters. But those who are dishonest in little matters will be dishonest with important matters" *Luke 16:10 CEV*.

Can you be trusted with what God has given to you? Can you be trusted with relationships? Can you be trusted with resources? Remember, God pays attention to even the smallest details, vs. 17. It is critical for all of us to be faithful managers of all that God entrust to us. This is especially true of our relationships and our resources.

Value and deem important those things God does. Love the Creator more than the created.

REFLECTIONS FROM LUKE 17

MINIATURE BUT MIGHTY

"*The apostles said to the Lord, Make our faith stronger!*"

Luke 17:5 CEV

Faith is powerful and can lead to abilities we could not imagine without the support of, and connection to an almighty God. *Hebrews 11* describes the awesome, miraculous, unbelievable feats accomplished by patriots, prophets and others in Old Testament scripture because of their faith.

When the disciples requested to have their faith made stronger, it was a surprise to hear Jesus' reply in *vs. 6*. If you have never seen a mustard seed, it is easy to describe, but not so easy to see. It is not just tiny, it is minuscule, and it is microscopic. One might consider it unimportant or insignificant as a result. However, Jesus says to have strong faith, mustard-seed-size is all you need. God distributes a certain amount of faith to everyone, (*Romans 12:3*). Everyone, even you and me, can have strong, crazy, powerful faith.

Luke 17 describes what we would be capable of with mustard seed, that is, tiny, miniscule, microscopic, faith.

- We would set better examples for others, *vs. 1-4.*

- We would serve with faithfulness and joy, *vs. 7-10.*

- We would express gratitude with regularity, *vs. 11-19.*

- We would get ready and stay ready to meet God, *vs. 22-37.*

Faith comes by hearing and by the Word of God, *Romans 10:17*. Our faith increase in these ways and more when we stay in God's Word. God desires us to be powerful and strong. When we stay in the Word, we inherit the power, to tear down the walls of racism and bigotry. This power then gives strength to build bridges that connect people. When we stay in the Word of God, we develop the energy to elevate the weak, the disenfranchised, the homeless, and the mentally ill. When we stay in the Word, we compassionately care for and spend time with the elderly, and our orphaned children. When we stay in the Word, we provide resources and support for the immigrant, the poor and any who are weak and powerless on their own.

When our faith becomes strong, we rise up on wings as eagles. We walk and do not become weary. We run and do not faint (see *Isaiah 40:31*). When our faith becomes strong, we stand firm, we hold fast, we endure to the end. Lord, make our faith stronger!

REFLECTIONS FROM LUKE 18

KEEP PRAYING

"Jesus told his disciples a story about how they should keep on praying and never give up:" Luke 81:1 CEV

Keep praying. There are times when I become weary, or doubtful. I am most tempted to give up on prayer in times like these. Jesus reminds His followers to keep praying.

- When It's seems like you will never have your request granted, keep praying, *vs. 2-8*

- When it seems like your flaws, mistakes and sins will prevent God from hearing you or forgiving you, keep praying, *vs. 9-14*

- When some would turn you away and say, "God doesn't have time for someone like you", keep praying, *vs. 15-17*

- When it seems like the sacrifice to stay connected to God is too great, keep praying, *vs. 18-34*

- When your prayer seems to be an annoyance, a bother or an inconvenience, keep praying, *vs. 35-43*

Whatever you do, do not stop praying. Pray when you are happy and blessed. Pray when you are down and sad. Pray when you have little. Pray when you have much. Pray when you feel like it. Pray when you do not feel like it. Do not stop praying.

In 1982, I received a phone call telling me my mother would not live throughout the night. I lived in Texas. She was a 14-hour car ride away. If I left to drive home at that very moment, I still would not make it home before morning. I began to pray. I prayed keep momma alive until morning. The next day came all to slow as I boarded a flight that would take me home. Once there I learned my mom was alive still. God heard and answered that prayer. So I kept praying. My next prayer was for God to save her life. Immediately, a physician they had trouble contacting arrived. He assessed my mom's situation and took her to surgery. My mom lived another 10 years. I kept praying. On another occasion while selling Christian magazines to earn money for college tuition, I knocked on the door of a certain home. It seemed no one was there at the time so I turned to go to the next house. That is when I saw what appeared to be a vicious dog. It was a Doberman Pinscher. I prayed, "Lord, I'm not going anywhere until he goes somewhere!" In a moment, a woman came to the door. I did not try to sell her a magazine, but did ask, "Is this your dog?" She replied, "Yes, but he doesn't bite." I thought in that moment, you might not have teeth, but he sure does. She commanded the dog to go to the back of the house and it obeyed. She then purchased two magazines.

Prayer is key in our relationship with God. God hears every prayer we pray. He also answers every prayer though not always in the way my two illustrations suggest. Our job is to keep on praying. God will hear and provide the right answer. Whatever you do, pray and do not give up.

REFLECTIONS FROM LUKE 19

LET HIM IN!

"The Son of Man came to look for and to save people who are lost." Luke 19:10 CEV

Clearly, there will always be people who will be critical of your decision to connect with God, *vs. 7*. The challenge is for you not to be one of those people. Do not hold your own self back or tie yourself down with negativity. Are you a sinner? Are you currently lost? If so, then it is for you and everyone like you that Jesus came to this world, *vs. 10.* He is looking for sinners.

Too many people hesitate using their gifts, talents and skills for God's glory all because they believe their sin disqualifies them from service. Every person God ever used was like you, a sinner. God is fully capable of taking care of sin. Your responsibility is to be faithful with whatever it is God has given you to use and to do. Use that, whatever it is, for His glory. Believe that God has called you to use your gifts and resources for Him regardless of what others may say or think. Remember, they criticized Jesus, but that did not stop Him from living out His purpose.

Do not sell yourself short. He will multiply your efforts, *vs. 11-27.*

Some will celebrate what you do, *vs. 28-40* and some will be so out of touch with God that they will attempt to stop you or even destroy what you are doing, *vs. 41-48.*

No matter who, no matter what, remember, He came to save you. Lost, broken, destitute, sick, blind, crippled, deaf, dumb, demon possessed, whatever the sin, He is searching for you. He wants to come to your house today. Therefore, whatever you are doing, stop and allow him access and entrance. Let Jesus come over. Let Him in. Stop and invite Him to come in today!

REFLECTIONS FROM LUKE 20

GOTCHA!

"Jesus' enemies could not catch him saying anything wrong there in front of the people. They were amazed at his answer and kept quiet." Luke 20:26

Luke 20 is replete with examples of religious people and the enemies of Jesus trying to trip Him up. They were determined to catch him in error. They hoped to push him into a circumstance where He would make a mistake. They even went to great lengths to set Him up to fail. They designed schemes and planned quizzes intended to trick and confuse Jesus. They were consistent and relentless in their efforts to prove that He was not a good person. They were determined to prove he was definitely not the Son of God.

There are two very important lessons to draw from *Luke 20*. First, no matter how much good you do, how many people you help, or how loving and kind you are, there will always be those who will want you to fail. Some will even work hard to ensure you fail. It does not make sense, but it is true - haters will hate and they will hate on even those who do good. People who hate God or hate His children will work for your destruction. Any mistake you make becomes an open the door to attacks. Errors and missteps become giant erasers to discount the good one has ever done. It is important to be aware that this was not just a challenge for Jesus, but will be a challenge for His followers. Like Jesus, be patient in dealing with such people. Be wise when dealing with such people. Keep doing good when dealing with such people. Rather than you, allow the Word of God to place such people in check, *vs. 8, 17, 21, 39*. In addition, most of all, whatever you do, do not be such people, *vs. 46, 47*.

Second, why do you read and study the Bible? Some do so only to prove they are right and that others are wrong. Some read to be able to point out the errors of others. *Luke 20* helps clarify that these are poor reason for studying the Word. Be motivated as you read scripture to allow what you read to help you to know and understand God better. To know God is to grow in your love for Him. The more you love Him the more you will love like Him. Loving like Him means loving those He loves. Throughout the book of Luke He makes it extremely clear that He loves sinners. When we love sinners, we will help and not hurt them. We will lift and not push them down. We will extend grace and not withhold forgiveness from them. We will not be trap setters trying to catch others doing wrong. We have a choice. We can be like Jesus or we can be like the religious tricksters. Choose today to be like Jesus.

REFLECTIONS FROM LUKE 21

EVERYTHING YOU HAVE

"Everyone else gave what they didn't need. But she is very poor and gave everything she had" Luke 21:4.

Luke 21 gives a vivid, graphic, detailed description of what the followers of Jesus could expect to face, vs. *5-35*. Being a disciple of God is not easy and requires a great deal more than you would imagine. T. Marshall Kelly, a

Gospel music baritone with a silky smooth voice, describes what it takes to be a disciple in the song, It Takes Everything to Serve the Lord. *"Some want a crown but they won't bear the cross, some want bright mansions but they won't pay the cost, some take His name while they still live in shame, some want to be seen but they don't want to be clean, it takes everything to serve the Lord." It takes your hands and your head and your heart yes you're all, it takes full surrender to serve the Lord and takes your time and your means and your prayers lest you fall it takes everything to serve the Lord."*

This woman in *Luke 21:4* gave what God requires. She gave all she had. Sure, some people gave more, if you only look at the amount. However, compared to what they had, what they gave was a mere donation. It was their pocket change. It was minuscule in comparison to God's blessings extended to them. When this woman gave, she had nothing left. It was everything she had. It might seem cruel that God would require everything from us. Stop for a moment and consider this; God never ask of us more than He has already done for us. In *Luke 21* Jesus begins his trek to the cross where He gives all. God gives all when He gave His Son Jesus, (See *John 3:16*). In response to God's great generosity, the widow gave all she had. The question is will you give all?

In human strength, sacrificial giving is impossible. *Vs. 36* instructs us to watch and pray. This is the key to successfully giving one's all. Watch, pay attention to all God had done and is doing for you. His mercies are new every morning. He gives 24/7 security and protective services. He provides the basic needs of food, water, shelter. He provides constant companionship. He does our spiritual laundry when He washes our sins and makes us clean and acceptable. If there were a charge for everything he did for us, how much would you owe? One songwriter put it this way, *"Jesus paid it all. All to Him I owe."*

REFLECTIONS FROM LUKE 22

DON'T BE SURPRISED

"Then they asked, "Are you the Son of God? Jesus answered, "You say I am!" Luke 22:70

What more evidence do we need? Jesus spoke with an authority that only comes from God. He taught lessons that made plain who He was and the way to salvation. He demonstrated the power of God when He healed the sick and those afflicted with conditions no human physician could cure. He fed multitudes, showing compassion for those who spent long days hearing parables and sermons that changed lives. He even raised the dead. He was the example, the pattern for how to do this life by faithfully praying, spending time alone with God, and treating others, especially known sinners, with love, acceptance and forgiveness. He is without question the Son of God.

After seeing and experiencing the life and ministry of Jesus, some still struggled with believing He was truly God's son. It surprised some that they were actually in the presence of God. To keep you from being surprised pay close attention to Luke 22. If it can happen to the Son of God, it can happen to His children.

- Do not be surprised when people close to you betray you or sell you out, *vs. 1-6.*

- Do not be surprised that God has worked out details for parts of your life that will amaze you, *vs. 7-13.*

- Do not be surprised by the lessons, symbolisms and insights you will gain by spending time with God, *vs. 14-20.*

- Do not be surprised when you begin to recognize who your adversaries are, but still treat them with love and respect anyway, *vs. 21-23, 47, 48.*

- Don't be surprised that greatness is revealed in servanthood, *vs. 24-30*

- Do not be surprised when you are tested and when you will fail miserably, *vs 31-34, 54-61.*

- Do not be surprised that some assignments given by God are very hard and require trusting God with everything, including your life, *vs. 42, 43.*

- Do not be surprised that prayer is the only way out of certain situations and if you do not pray, you are destined to fail, *vs. 39, 45.*

- Do not be surprised when you have spent time in prayer and in consistent Bible study, that you will develop boldness and lose fear.

- Do not be surprised that you will proclaim God with Confidence.

- Do not be surprised that you will have a sweet assurance of your eternal place, *vs. 66-70.*

Jesus is the Son of God. Allow Him to be God in and over your life. When you do this, don't be surprised by everything that will happen. Whatever happens, good or bad, have confidence that He is the Son of God. Know that He is with you always. Know and believe that He will see you through.

REFLECTIONS FROM LUKE 23

YOU KNOW TOO

"A crowd had gathered to see the terrible sight. Then after they had seen it, they felt brokenhearted and went home." Luke 23:48 CEV

The Chief Priest knew, the religious leaders knew, the people in the crowd knew, Pilate knew, Herod knew, the two thieves executed with Jesus knew, the soldiers who executed Him knew. They all knew, liked we all know, Jesus is the Son of God, *vs. 1-17, 39-43, 47.* When you are faithful to take inventory of your life, the things you've seen, heard and experienced, you will know for yourself that someone greater than you was involved in all the intricate details. It is extremely difficult, upon review, not to see God. You will find that He is in the good experiences of life as well as the painful experiences. Knowing that He has been with you will increase your confidence that He will be with you moving forward. The Christian experience is not void of pain, trauma or difficulty. I have found that it is in the darkest of times God draws closest. He is more recognizable in the darkest times when we are intentional about acquainting ourselves with Him in times of ease and light. Dark times will come. Know that God will be there. He will not leave you or forsake you (Hebrews 13:5). This you must know.

> *"Around noon the sky turned dark and stayed that way until the middle of the afternoon." Luke 23:44 CEV*

The power of darkness is great. It causes people to act and to behave contrary to what they know is good and right. Many of the people in the crowd who called out for Jesus' crucifixion were witnesses to the miracles He performed. Some of the crowd themselves had been healed by Jesus. They heard with their own ears the sermons, parables and lessons He shared. He physically fed them. They recently cheered Him as he made His way into Jerusalem (*Luke 19:35-40*). Now they shout and demand that Jesus be executed, *vs. 18, 23.*

- When the power of darkness is in control, truth is of no consequence. Lies are told to establish reasons for the wrong that is being done, *vs. 2, 5, 10, 23-17.*

- When the power of darkness is in control injustice and maltreatment prevails, *vs. 11, 17, 22, 24-26, 36-39.*

- When the power if darkness is in control we gamble and take chances unwise to take, *vs. 34, 35.*

> "They said, "If you are the king of the Jews, save yourself!"" *Luke 23:37 CEV*

Jesus understood His purpose for coming into this world. It was not to save Himself, but to save us. Those that chided Him were clueless that His staying on the cross revealed the greater act of being King. His commitment to endure the cross and despise the shame was the greater display of his power. Jesus is the Light in the darkness.

- John 1:5

- John 8:12

Jesus is the Savior of the world.

- John 3:16

A decision for Jesus brings life, joy and peace. A decision against Him creates broken heartedness. It may seem good in the moment to side against Jesus, but after that moment has elapsed, you become faced with sad realities enshrouded in darkness. The crowd who gathered at the crucifixion felt this reality. They were broken-hearted. They went home empty, sad and lost (*vs. 48).*

Jesus prayed for strength to go through this time of darkness (*Luke 22:39-46).* He did not save Himself. He saved us. As with Barabbas, Jesus died to set free, (*vs 18, 19, 24).*

When you decided to walk in the Light with Jesus, some will distance themselves from you, (*vs. 49).* Some will tell lies on you. So will seek to crucify you. When these things happen, do as Jesus did. Pray and forgive, (*vs. 34).* Place yourself in God's hands, (*vs. 46).* It may seem like a dark time but know that Sabbath rest follows your dark day and difficult times (*vs. 56).* When crucified remember this is Friday. Rest on Sabbath, be still and be patient. Hold on, your resurrection is coming!

REFLECTIONS FROM LUKE 24

DOUBT DISPELLED

"They said to each other, "When he talked with us along the road and explained the Scriptures to us, didn't it warm our hearts?"" Luke 24:32 CEV

Early Sunday morning, when the women who returned to the tomb of Jesus to complete the preparation of the body for burial, they discovered He was not in the tomb, (*vs. 1-4).* Peter ran to the tomb also finding it empty. The only thing he found were the grave clothes Jesus wore, (*vs. 12).* Word of the empty tomb quickly circulated among the followers of Jesus. Cleopas and another disciple discussed the empty tomb as they travelled to the village of Emmas. All the followers of Jesus seemed troubled and confused by the empty tomb, (*vs. 17-25*). Trouble and confusion are the children of doubt. When you lose confidence in God's Word, you conceive trouble and confusion. When you forget what you have studied and heard from the Word of God, you give birth to trouble and confusion. When you live as if the Word of God has no power and authority in your life, you nurture and raise up trouble and confusion.

When we stay connected to God and His Word, when we faithfully trust what He says, when we live out the Word of God with confidence, trouble and confusion are no longer a concern. Jesus told His followers in advance what would happen, (*vs. 6, 7*). He took them back to the Word of God to show them once more that those things He shared and taught was absolutely true and could be trusted, (*vs. 27, 44*).

Trouble and confusion are powerful and convincing siblings. Even after testimonials by the women who spoke with an angel at the tomb, after testimonials by disciples who walked, talked and dined with the risen Savior, and even after Jesus' appearance before them in the very room they were in, they were still troubled and confused, (*vs. 37, 38*).

Much will happen in your life as a disciple of God that will trouble and confuse you if you forget or when you doubt God's Word. The Word of God, when believed, gives birth to faith, confidence, hope, happiness, joy, peace and praise, (*vs. 32, 41, 52, 53*). The offspring of faith and belief are amazing, effective and powerful. To give birth to belief one must stay close to the Savior. One must stay constant in the Word and in prayer. It will take revisiting the Word, (*vs. 45-49*), to be clear in understanding what God desires of you. The Word of God will not only remove doubt that causes trouble and confusion; it will not only produce hope, happiness, joy, peace and praise; the Word will also give you the power and confidence to proclaim Good News of a risen Savior to a troubled and dying world. Each of us has the assignment to proclaim the Word of God. It is a blessed privilege to proclaim this Good News, (*vs. 50*). Believe His Word and never doubt.

FINAL REFLECTION FROM LUKE

"But Mary kept thinking about all this and wondering what it meant." Luke 2:19 CEV

Keep on thinking about what you are reading and discovering from God's Word. Keep on contemplating on the Word to understand what it means for you personally. All of scripture is rich in resources that will lead you to salvation. God's Spirit enlightens, inspires and reveals marvelous insight to all who keep on meditating on the life of Jesus. Do not be discouraged and give up when you do not understand things, keep reading. There is fresh manna waiting for you.

REFLECTIONS ON
THE BOOK OF JOHN

BEGINNING AT THE BEGINNING

In the beginning was the Word and the Word was with God and
The Word was God. The same was in the beginning with God'
John 1:1-2 KJV

John's gospel begins with a bombshell, as he pens his gospel he makes emphatic statements about Jesus.

First, that He was here in the beginning and He was always with God (the Father) and was the architect of everything that exists. Second, that life was in Jesus and that that life was the light of the world.

John opens his gospel by presenting the origin of Jesus as definitive fact. This is a departure from his eyewitness account of the ministry of Jesus. John reminds us that faith as well as being an eyewitness, is the foundation of his account of Jesus and His ministry.

"The substance of things hoped for the evidence of things not seen" Hebrews 11:1 KJV

To begin his experience, John introduces faith as a companion to his eyewitness account. As I consider a contrasting theory of the origin of the universe like the scientific Big Bang Theory. It might take more faith to accept the scientific concept of (a random explosion that produces complex micro and macro order that continues for billions of years uninterrupted that produces the order of our current environment including the complexity of man), but I digress. Here is my point! Usually when someone makes a statement this emphatic, it almost always comes from a place of complete confidence. No speculation, accusation or arrogance, but rather supreme confidence without the fear of contradiction.

When I read John's opening statement I am immediately transported into the realm of concrete assurance. John is guiding me into an absolute truth. He is saying this is not what I think or what most believe, John is saying, here are the facts, plain, uncut, without fear of contradiction, so deal with it! This kind of an approach immediately gains my attention if not my outright respect. It is also a departure from the style and approach of the first three Gospel's, Matthew Mark and Luke. I now see why John's gospel is not considered a Synoptic of the first three Gospels. John is not just attempting to relay a story; he is telling it as he experienced it. Just like the iconic character Detective Joe Friday from the 1950's television series Dragnet. John seems to say just like Detective Joe Friday "just the facts mam just the facts"

As I think about John's style and approach in his account of the life, influence and ministry of Jesus, I see a holy boldness in John, a kind of boldness that was not on display by any Apostle until after the day of Pentecost. Sure, Peter was brash, Nathanael was dismissive Thomas doubted. Even after following Jesus for three and a half years, witnessing the miracles he performed. They still were not quite sure about Jesus, Then came Pentecost.

At the beginning of his account of Jesus's public ministry John goes right for the jugular, John says, sit up take notice, here's who we're dealing with and here's how it happened. Chapter one jumps right into the beginning of Jesus's public ministry by introducing us to a man named John who preached in the wilderness, not in the synagogue or by the sea shore or by a hillside, not even in the town's limits. John held his meetings in the wilderness. Think about that, John was so compelling in his preaching of the coming Messiah, that people would come out to the wilderness to hear what he had to say. Do not lose me on this one; it was the wilderness. The wilderness was called the wilderness because it was not safe; it was also hard to traverse. The wilderness probably had dangerous animals and unmanageable people hence the designation *Wilde*rness. However, John had the people's attention despite the obvious dangers.

John was a true leader. How do I know? Because he had followers. Not like Facebook, Instagram or Twitter, John had disciples, they followed him spoke on his behalf and most of all supported him with their presence. Do you understand what I mean? Leaders are people who have other people following them, thus LEADer.

John had an unusual style and appearance but his unorthodox style drew people to him. John had conviction. John preached with so much conviction that the Jews sent priest and Levites to the wilderness, all the way from Jerusalem to ask whether he was the Christ or a prophet. Each inquiry into his own importance gave the forerunner of Christ more fuel for the fire that burned within him to "make straight the way of the Lord." John left no doubt to whoever would listen that he was not the Messiah. In fact John made the issue so clear that he confessed he was not even worthy to take off one string of the Messiah's sandals. Because John had the attention and support of the people, his elevation of the one who would come after him made the Jewish religious leaders very nervous. I am sure they were concerned about the coming Messiah. By the time John finished assuring the people that one greater than he was coming, I imagine the Jewish Leaders were anxious to see if indeed this man John, who baptized people by immersing them under the water was truly a man sent by God, or just a strange bewildering character.

Then it happened, the next day, Jesus appeared walking directly towards John the timing was perfect as John's eyes met the form of Jesus the Baptist cried out *"Behold the Lamb of God which taketh away the sin of the world" John 1:29 KJV*. What a relief, finally what John the Baptist had preached for so long in the wilderness he now beheld with his own eyes. He could finally direct the people's attention to the Messiah.

When Jesus came to see John, he desired that John would baptize him. Jesus' need to be baptized was a bewildering request. Baptism was taught and accepted as a spiritual rite for the believer. Baptism is making a public confession to burying an old life of sin to walk in the new light of righteous. However, Jesus had no sin to confess. He was perfect and upright and was without blemish. So why chose baptism? Jesus chose to be baptized to validate John's ministry and the method of immersion. What a fulfillment. What a culmination of John's effort now made manifest unto all Israel.

The Messiah was here!

REFLECTIONS FROM JOHN 2

A CONFLUENCE OF MIRACLES

Jesus had been baptized in the Jordan River by John the Baptist and had begun to assemble his disciples. It was the third day, and there was a marriage in Cana of Galilee. Jesus's mother was there and Jesus and his disciples were invited to the marriage. It is interesting to note that the scripture reads,

> *"And when they wanted wine the mother of Jesus said to Jesus they have no wine" John 2:3 KJV.*

This passage has often been seen as a confirmation for the use of alcoholic beverages. Many conclude that if Jesus converted water into wine for the benefit of a wedding party, then it is permissible for Disciples of Christ. It is interesting to look objectively at this passage, and when we do, we will see the exact same thing that Jesus saw. Here is what I mean, stay with me. I am almost in a state of disbelief that sincere followers of Jesus could conclude that the Messiah would provide an intoxicating beverage to the very people he came to save. John emphatically writes in chapter one verse four and five. *"In Him was life; and the life was the light of men and the light shineth in darkness; and the darkness comprehended it not" John 1:4, 5 KJV.* This subject on the use of alcoholic beverages or as it is commonly referred to today "adult beverages" has produced some of the darkest periods in the history of the United States, even the world. Go with me to the 1820's and 30's more than 40 years before the American Civil War. A wave of religious revivalism swept across America, leading to increased calls for temperance and state laws banning the sale of alcohol (spirits). This period also lead to the Abolitionist Movement to end slavery. Alcohol was seen as a destructive force in families and marriages, and was considered the cause of most corruption, poverty and crime in America. This period was a very dark time for the nation. Almost 100 years after the temperance movements began, on January 16 1919 The United States Congress enacted the 18th amendment to the constitution to outlaw the sale of alcohol. The Volstead Act was produced on October 28th 1919 to provide enforcement for the 18 Amendment, Prohibiting the manufacture, sale and distribution of alcoholic beverages The 66th Congress of the United States HR6810. As of Today the 18 amendment to the U.S. Constitution is the only amendment ever repealed.

By 1933, the Great Depression and organized crime had all but eliminated opposition to the use of alcohol. Franklin Delano Roosevelt, a Democratic candidate for President of the United States, ran on a platform that guaranteed the repeal of prohibition. FDR, as he was called by many, won the presidency in a landslide over Republican candidate Herbert Hoover who campaigned in support of prohibition. FDR took office on March 4, 1933. The 21st Amendment to the Constitution of the United States, which repealed the 18th amendment, was ratified on December 5 1933, (U.S. Constitution). Alcohol once again flowed legally in the streets of America.

Now what does this period of American history have to do with John 1 verses 4 and 5? *"And the light shineth in darkness and the darkness comprehended it not"*. The religious awakening of the 1830's produced Temperance Movements and the elimination of the use of alcohol. Those reform movements helped expose the evils in American society that were actually ripping the fabric of the American family apart. Light shined on the darkness but the darkness comprehended it not. As we consider where we are today. According to the National Institute on Alcohol Abuse. On average eighty eight Thousand Americans (88,000) die every year from alcohol related causes, (Source: The National Institute of Health). This makes alcohol one of the leading causes of preventable death in the U.S.

Alcohol is causally linked to more than 200 different diseases, conditions, and injuries (as specified in the *International Classification of Diseases, Revision 10 Source :NIH.*

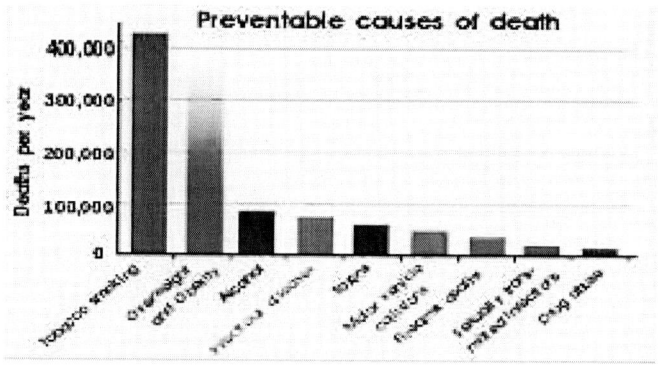

World War 2 was, and still is the deadliest war in the history of the United States. Over the six-year period from 1939 to 1945, The U.S. lost Four Hundred and Nineteen Thousand Soldiers (419,000), Source: The National Archives. Over a six year period from 2014 to 2019 The U.S. has lost Five Hundred Twenty Eight Thousand (528,000) Men Women and children to Alcohol related causes, Source: National Institute of Health. What does any of this have to do with Jesus's first miracle? I am glad you asked. The word "wine" translated into Greek from Hebrew is "Yayin". A more accurate translation to English might read. *John 2 verse 3 "and when yayin was lacking the mother of Jesus says to Him, they do not have yayin."* In Hebrew "yayin" means freshly pressed non-fermented juice. The Hebrew and Greek word for fermented or alcohol is "oinos". The definition for Oinos is, "wine that is foaming", it is derived from the root "Hamar" which means to boil up or is fermented. Fermentation is the chemical process of the decomposition of the sugars in the fruit. When fructose (sugar) decomposes or becomes rotten, the rotting sugar converts into ethanol. Ethanol's primary uses area Solvent in varnishes and perfume, a preservative for biological specimens, in the preparation of essences and flavorings in many medicines and drugs, as a disinfectant and as fuel and gasoline additive. In essence, ethanol is a toxic chemical. According to the United States Department of Justice, The Bureau of Alcohol Tobacco Firearms and Explosives is a law enforcement agency tasked with the responsibility of controlling dangerous substances in America.

Isn't it interesting that alcohol is grouped with tobacco, guns and explosives?

In this story of Jesus's first miracle, the word used by John in every reference to wine is "Yayin" and the word "Oinos" is never used.

The Great English playwright William Shakespeare speaks to us from the character Cassio in the tragedy named Othello.

> "I remember a mass of things, but nothing distinctly. A quarrel, but nothing wherefore. Oh, that men should put an enemy in their mouths to steal away their brains! That we should,

with joy, pleasance revel and applause, transform ourselves into beasts", (William Shakespeare's Othello)!

^{29}*But I say unto you, I will not drink henceforth of this fruit of the vine, until that day when I drink it new with you in my Father's kingdom. Matthew 26:29 KJV*

There it is, right there in front of you, can you see it, Light.

REFLECTIONS FROM JOHN 2 CONTINUED

"MERCH IN THE CHURCH"

Jesus had just completed his first miracle turning water into wine. Passover was soon to begin so Jesus his mother and his disciples began their journey up to Jerusalem. When Jesus arrived at Jerusalem the scripture records, he found in the temple those that sold oxen and sheep and doves and money-changers sitting. Jesus didn't question anyone about this practice; he didn't lament over the scene the scripture records that he began to make a small whip and drove the offenders out while turning over the tables and casting the money to the floor. Then Jesus proclaimed,

> *"don't make my father's house a house of merchandise. Then His disciples remembered it is written, the zeal of thine house hath eaten me up", John 2:16, 17 NKJV.*

Wow! What do you think drove Jesus to act on this scene rather than ask questions about the practice. Wouldn't it be prudent to first check with those in charge of the temple to verify if the sellers of sacrifices and the moneychangers had permission to sell and exchange. After all, weren't they providing a needed service to the temple by making sure the people had what was required in order to sacrifice? Was Jesus out of order, after all, he had just arrived in Jerusalem for Passover, what gave him the authority to take control over a temple that was not his responsibility?

In my role as a Media Consultant and Systems Integrator, I travel around the country interacting with churches and ministries of various denomination's and customs. I witness this practice of selling merchandise and exchanging money for services still today. From a Pumpkin Spice Iced Frappuccino to CD's, books to bibles, hats to houseware, often right in the sanctuary. As I consider these practices, my mind is drawn to this statement.

"Never, never be afraid to do what's right, especially if the well-being of a person or animal is at stake. Society's punishments are small compared to the wounds we inflict on our soul when we look the other way." —Author Unknown.

Do you remember how John started his account of Jesus's public ministry?

3 *"All things were made by him; and without him was not anything made that was made. 4In him was life; and the life was the light of men. 5And the light shineth in darkness; and the darkness comprehended it not". John 1:3-5 KJV*

9 *"For the zeal of thine house hath eaten me up; and the reproaches of them that reproached thee are fallen upon me". Psalm 69:9.KJV*

It was then that his disciples remembered that the scripture said these words; it was then that they understood. Do you understood?

The Jews confronted Jesus and insisted that he show them some sign that would prove his right to drive out the merchants.

Jesus responds to the question by making one of the most astonishing claims ever! Jesus responded,

"Destroy this temple, and I will raise it again in three days."

John 2:19 KJV.

This answer utterly confounded the Jews. They said, it took 46 years to build the temple and you will rebuild it in three days?

Question: What was the purpose of the Temple?

Answer: To house the altar were sacrifice for sin was offered

God required a Sacrifice for the remission of sin.

11 *For the life of the flesh is in the blood: and I have given it to you upon the altar to make an atonement for your souls:*

for it is the blood that maketh an atonement for the soul.
Leviticus 17:11 KJV

"All we like sheep have gone astray; we have turned every one
to his own way; and the Lord hath laid on him the iniquity of
us all. [7]He was oppressed, and he was afflicted, yet he opened
not his mouth: he is brought as a lamb to the slaughter, and
as a sheep before her shearers is dumb, so he openeth not his
mouth". Isaiah 53:6, 7 KJV

[2]Hear, O heavens, and give ear, O earth: for the Lord hath
spoken, I have nourished and brought up children, and they
have rebelled against me. [3]The ox knoweth his owner, and the
ass his master's crib: but Israel doth not know, my people doth
not consider. [4]Ah sinful nation, a people laden with iniquity,
a seed of evildoers, children that are corrupters: they have
forsaken the Lord, they have provoked the Holy One of Israel
unto anger, they are gone away backward. Isaiah 1:2-4 KJV

Do you remember *John 1:29*?

"Behold the Lamb of God which taketh away the sin of
the world"

Jesus is the perfect sacrifice that the temple rite stood for in Type and anti-type. The Old Testament prophet Isaiah prophesied it, and now John was witnessing it.

There it is again, Light, can you see it?

REFLECTIONS ON JOHN 3

THE ORIGINAL NICK AT NIGHT

Six media conglomerates are referred to as the big six. This big six produce and manage almost all the media produced in the world.

1. National Amusements

2. The Disney Corporation

3. Time Warner

4. Comcast

5. Newscorp

6. Sony Corporation

The influence of these conglomerates reach into every aspect of life. From what we watch to entertain ourselves, to what we believe to be the news reports that concern us, even how rapidly we are able to communicate with those around us both near and far. In this digital age, mobile devices are the dominant tool of our time. Nevertheless, the question is! Are we really communicating or are we just expressing ourselves? Does the capacity of gigabit storage and 5G bandwidth only speed up our distance from each other and meaningful dialog?

Nicodemus was a Jewish religious leader. As a member of the Sanhedrin, he was held in high esteem. Therefore, when he sought the council of Jesus, he placed his position and status at risk.

The Jewish leadership was determined to kill Jesus and dispose of him so that no one would remember what he said or did.

However, Nicodemus was convinced although not convicted, that Jesus was indeed someone special. So in order to not arouse any suspicion among the Sanhedrin he sought a private meeting with Jesus at night. Nicodemus was careful in how he approached the savior so he begins by offering Jesus platitudes. "Rabbi, we know that thou art a teacher come from God; for no man can do these miracles that thou doest, except God be with him. *John 3:2 KJV*

Now here is where the fun starts! Jesus answered Nicodemus by saying

> *"Verily Verily I say unto thee except a man be born again he cannot enter the kingdom of heaven" John 3:3 KJV*

Nicodemus say's I believe that God is with you. Jesus says you cannot enter the kingdom of heaven unless you are born again.

What Jesus does with his response is, cut to the chase. Jesus reads the intent of Nicodemus and cuts him off by not entertaining his platitude. Then the words "verily verily".

Whenever you see Jesus repeat his words you are about to get the hard, uncut straight truth. No sugar, no medicine no parable just TRUTH so deal with it. Nicodemus's response is classic failure, Not only did he not understand Jesus's response; he did not understand that Jesus was schooling him.

Look at this exchange:

"Nicodemus saith unto him, how can a man be born when he is old? Can he enter the second time into his mother's womb, and be born? Jesus answered, verily, verily, I say unto thee, except a man be born of water and of the spirit, he cannot enter into the kingdom of God. 6 That which is born of the flesh is flesh; and that which is born of the Spirit is spirit. John 3:4-6KJV

HERE IT IS! Do not miss this; Jesus is describing here the key element that distinguishes sinful man from spiritual man.

The rebirth process transforms the person born in sin and shaped in iniquity into a spirit lead person with new desires and tendencies that are sensitive to the guidance of the spirit not driven by the lust of the flesh. Jesus continues:

[7]Marvel not that I said unto thee, Ye must be born again. [8]The wind bloweth where it listeth, and thou hearest the sound thereof, but canst not tell whence it cometh, and whither it goeth: so is every one that is born of the Spirit. [9]Nicodemus answered and said unto him, How can these things be? [10]Jesus answered and said unto him, Art thou a master of Israel, and knowest not these things?

Herein lies one of the world's greatest tragedies, Jesus confronts Nicodemus with the ironic reality of spiritual leadership in the world today.

Here it is, spiritual leadership devoid of the controlling influence of the Spirit of God is imminent death. Isn't that ironic, those who present themselves as representatives of God are often devoid of the very Spirit they claim to possess.

This irony suggests that in God's masterplan for the redemption of His children, He has devised a process that is secure, uninterruptible and hack proof.

It is called THE HOLY SPIRIT! God gives the Holy Spirit to those who sincerely desire to be lead. Never does God grant the controlling power of His Spirit to be used under the control of sinful men. Unlike the media conglomerates, God is not entertaining the world He is saving it. Because of Nicodemus' ignorance to this, Jesus concludes.

> [11]*Verily, verily, I say unto thee, We speak that we do know, and testify that we have seen; and ye receive not our witness.* [12]*If I have told you earthly things, and ye believe not, how shall ye believe, if I tell you of heavenly things? KJV*

Jesus is not playing games with Nicodemus He's delivering the straight Gospel and this exchange leads us into probably the most recognized promise in all of scripture.

> [16]*For God so loved the world, that he gave his only begotten Son, that whosoever believeth in him should not perish, but have everlasting life.* [17]*For God sent not his Son into the world to condemn the world; but that the world through him might be saved.* [18]*He that believeth on him is not condemned: but he that believeth not is condemned already, because he hath not believed in the name of the only begotten Son of God.* [19]*And this is the condemnation, that light is come into the world, and men loved darkness rather than light, because their deeds were evil. John 3:16-19 KJV*

There it is again! Do you see it now! Light!

REFLECTIONS ON JOHN 4

THE ELIXIR OF LIFE

As Jesus continues his travels, he comes to a place that is significant in the history of the Jewish people, "Jacobs Well"

> [5]*Then cometh he to a city of Samaria, which is called Sychar, near to the parcel of ground that Jacob gave to his son Joseph.*

⁶Now Jacob's well was there. Jesus therefore, being wearied with his journey, sat thus on the well: and it was about the sixth hour. ⁷There cometh a woman of Samaria to draw water: Jesus saith unto her, Give me to drink. ⁸(For his disciples were gone away unto the city to buy meat.) John 4:6-8 KJV

Before we look at what happens at Jacobs Well, it's important to note the scripture say's in verse eight, the disciples went into the city to buy meat. The word here translated "Meat" is the Hebrew word "Okhel" which means food. A more accurate translation of this passage would be" For his disciples were gone into town to buy food". This reference does not suggest that the disciples went to buy the flesh of dead animals. This is an important distinction. By its practical and prophetic definition, meat is food, or the heart of a food substance (i.e. heart of a tomato, or an almond or a potato,) not the flesh of animal products. The reason I magnify this passage is because, I am convinced that our reading of God's word MUST be done in the context of studying what God has to say, not simply reading what is written. And in our study we confirm the word of God

"¹⁵Study to shew thyself approved unto God, a workman that needeth not to be ashamed, rightly dividing the word of truth". 2Timothy 2:15 KJV

More on this later.

At Jacobs well, Jesus encounters a woman. This interaction was unusual because the woman happened to be a Samaritan.

Samaritans were considered to be beneath Jews, which made interaction between the two cultures meaningless.

But Jesus was not hindered by tradition, dogmas or rituals. Jesus lived above the constraints of human society, as if in the light of divine presence. Indeed, he was not a mere messenger he was the Messiah! Therefore, as Jesus asked for a drink of water, the woman was astonished that a Jew would speak to her let alone ask for something from her. Although Jesus was thirsty, drinking water was not the only thing on his mind.

"Jesus answered and said unto her, If thou knewest the gift of God, and who it is that saith to thee, Give me to drink; thou

wouldest have asked of him, and he would have given thee
living water. John 4:10 KJV

With this statement, Jesus completely dismantled the notion that salvation was of the Jews. It was his intention to share the good news of the gospel with whoever would receive it. Water was a good analogy for his interaction with her, and Jesus used this analogy to reveal his mission. However, the woman was not easily persuaded, she sought to challenge Jesus's statement that he had a source of water he called living water. Therefore, she reminded Jesus that if he was going to provide water he would first need a bucket and something to draw the water up with, and the well was deep. In addition, with almost an irony in her voice she says, are you going to produce this living water? Are you greater than Jacob who gave us the well and drank from it as well and his sons and cattle? Oh, by the way, you were just asking me for water!

> *Jesus answered and said unto her, Every one that drinketh*
> *of this water shall thirst again: 14 but whosoever drinketh*
> *of the water that I shall give him shall never thirst; but the*
> *water that I shall give him shall become in him a well of water*
> *springing up unto eternal life. John 4:13-14 KJV*

Once again Jesus has changed the focus, from the physical to the spiritual, from natural to supernatural. Just the nature of his voice and the power of his words the woman at the well now wants more! The woman saith unto him,

> *Sir, give me this water, that I thirst not, neither come all the*
> *way hither to draw verse 15 KJV.*

At this point, the woman is willing to experience a change, so Jesus helps her to take the plunge.

> [16]*Jesus saith unto her, Go, call thy husband, and come hither.*
> [17]*The woman answered and said unto him, I have no husband. Jesus saith unto her, Thou saidst well, I have no husband:* [18]*for thou hast had five husbands; and he whom thou now hast is not thy husband: this hast thou said truly.*
> *John 4:16-18 KJV*

Was Jesus attempting to condemn and embarrass her? Not at all, remember when the woman reminded him that he did not have anything with which he could draw water! Here is his bucket:

> *Jesus saith unto her, Woman, believe me, the hour cometh, when neither in this mountain, nor in Jerusalem, shall ye worship the Father. [22]Ye worship that which ye know not: we worship that which we know; for salvation is from the Jews. [23]But the hour cometh, and now is, when the true worshippers shall worship the Father in spirit and truth: [g]for such doth the Father seek to be his worshippers. [24][h]God is a Spirit: and they that worship him must worship in spirit and truth. [25]The woman saith unto him, I know that Messiah cometh (he that is called Christ): when he is come, he will declare unto us all things. [26]Jesus saith unto her, I that speak unto thee am he. John 4:21-26 KJV*

This passage of scripture is loaded with truths that redefine what it means to connect with God and the very nature of God. However, of all the fascinating truths that Jesus reveals, is his confession to her that **"I Am the Messiah ".** WOW! The woman at the well got what Jesus had promised, living water springing up and her response was: *Come, see a man, who told me all things that ever* I did: can this be the Christ? *John 4:29 KJV*

> *And from that city many of the Samaritans believed on him because of the word of the woman, who testified, He told me all things that ever* I did. [40]*So when the Samaritans came unto him, they besought him to abide with them: and he abode there two days. [41]And many more believed because of his word; [42]and they said to the woman, Now we believe, not because of thy speaking: for we have heard for ourselves, and know that this is indeed the Saviour of the world. John 4:39-42 KJV*

Here is a new Equation for you!

PG + PT= SS

The power of God plus the power of a testimony equals saved souls

JESUS THE TROUBLEMAKER

How ironic is it that according to some, doing good can be in violation of what's good. That's not ironic it's idiotic, there I said it. Now that I have gotten that off my chest, you are probably wondering what in the world am I talking about. Look here at this story and see if you agree with me.

> *After this there was a feast of the Jews; and Jesus went up to Jerusalem. ²Now there is at Jerusalem by the sheep market a pool, which is called in the Hebrew tongue Bethesda, having five porches. ³In these lay a great multitude of impotent folk, of blind, halt, withered, waiting for the moving of the water. ⁴For an angel went down at a certain season into the pool, and troubled the water: whosoever then first after the troubling of the water stepped in was made whole of whatsoever disease he had. ⁵And a certain man was there, which had an infirmity thirty and eight years. ⁶When Jesus saw him lie, and knew that he had been now a long time in that case, he saith unto him, Wilt thou be made whole? ⁷The impotent man answered him, Sir, I have no man, when the water is troubled, to put me into the pool: but while I am coming, another steppeth down before me. ⁸Jesus saith unto him, Rise, take up thy bed, and walk. ⁹And immediately the man was made whole, and took up his bed, and walked: and on the same day was the sabbath.¹⁰The Jews therefore said unto him that was cured, It is the sabbath day: it is not lawful for thee to carry thy bed. ¹¹He answered them, He that made me whole, the same said unto me, Take up thy bed, and walk. ¹²Then asked they him, What man is that which said unto thee, Take up thy bed, and walk? John 5:1-12 KJV*

This story is an amazing reflection on where we are today.

The religious leaders were upset that a man received healing after thirty-eight long years, only because he carried his bed on the Sabbath. I could go on and on about the absurdity of this one but that would give too much airtime to the tripe!

Here is what you need to know!

> ^{13}*And he that was healed wist not who it was: for Jesus had conveyed himself away, a multitude being in that place. ^{14}Afterward Jesus findeth him in the temple, and said unto him, Behold, thou art made whole: sin no more, lest a worse thing come unto thee. ^{15}The man departed, and told the Jews that it was Jesus, which had made him whole. ^{16}And therefore did the Jews persecute Jesus, and sought to slay him, because he had done these things on the sabbath day. ^{17}But Jesus answered them, My Father worketh hitherto, and I work. ^{18}Therefore the Jews sought the more to kill him, because he not only had broken the sabbath, but said also that God was his Father, making himself equal with God. John 5:13-18 KJV*

This is what we produce when we put profits over people and systems over salvation. Are you a lawbreaker? Think about that!

REFLECTIONS ON JOHN 6

HEY, DON'T WE KNOW YOU!

As Jesus continues his ministry, he crosses over the Sea of Galilee and there are multitudes of people following him. They had witnesses the miracles that Jesus performed and were now following him probably to see what would happen next.

When Jesus sees the great multitude, he suggests to his disciples that they find bread to feed the people. The following text alludes to the sense of humor the Messiah possessed. Jesus asks the question not seeking a solution, but to challenge the disciple's faith. The text says that Jesus already knew what he would do.

Prior to this situation in every instance of need, Jesus performed miracles without the assistance or input from his disciples. This was the main reason they were facing a multitude the people witnessed for themselves the miracles of the messiah.

Jesus was trusting in his father to supply their need; he was not placing trust or confidence in human solutions. Jesus was producing results! Jesus was setting the stage for is next miracle!

⁵When Jesus then lifted up his eyes, and saw a great company come unto him, he saith unto Philip, Whence shall we buy bread, that these may eat? ⁶And this he said to prove him: for he himself knew what he would do. ⁷Philip answered him, Two hundred pennyworth of bread is not sufficient for them, that every one of them may take a little. ⁸One of his disciples, Andrew, Simon Peter's brother, saith unto him, ⁹There is a lad here, which hath five barley loaves, and two small fishes: but what are they among so many? John 6:5-9 KJV

Really, Andrew! Did you not just witness the healing of the man by the pool of Bethesda what about when Jesus just spoke the word and the noblemen's son was healed, certainly, you remember the water into wine, you drank that miracle for yourself! Now you say five loves and two small fish is not enough!

Before you jump on the bandwagon condemning Andrew for his doubt, isn't he really just a symbol of all of us. If you just look back over your own life, hasn't God already done enough in each of our lives to foster a level of trust in Him beyond the circumstances that confront us? ***Raise your hand! Confession noted!***

Now watch Jesus go to work!

¹⁰And Jesus said, Make the men sit down. Now there was much grass in the place. So the men sat down, in number about five thousand. ¹¹And Jesus took the loaves; and when he had given thanks, he distributed to the disciples, and the disciples to them that were set down; and likewise of the fishes as much as they would. ¹²When they were filled, he said unto his disciples, Gather up the fragments that remain, that nothing be lost. ¹³Therefore they gathered them together, and filled twelve baskets with the fragments of the five barley loaves, which remained over and above unto them that had eaten. ¹⁴Then those men, when they had seen the miracle that Jesus did, said, This is of a truth that prophet that should come into the world. ¹⁵When Jesus therefore perceived that they would come and take him by force, to make him a king, he departed again into a mountain himself alone. John 6:10-15 KJV

It's wonderfully amazing to watch Jesus minister to people and still maintain the integrity of the purpose for which he came into the world. Jesus avoided the peoples draft to make him King.

As the people experienced Jesus feeding thousands with five loaves and two fish, they questioned in their hearts, if Jesus can feed thousands he could also feed an army. If he can feed an army, we can liberate ourselves from the oppressive Romans.

However, the master did not come to establish an earthly kingdom; his mission was to do the will of His Father who was indeed King of the Universe!

32Then Jesus said unto them, Verily, verily, I say unto you, Moses gave you not that bread from heaven; but my Father giveth you the true bread from heaven. 33For the bread of God is he which cometh down from heaven, and giveth life unto the world. 34Then said they unto him, Lord, evermore give us this bread. 35And Jesus said unto them, I am the bread of life: he that cometh to me shall never hunger; and he that believeth on me shall never thirst. 36But I said unto you, That ye also have seen me, and believe not. 37All that the Father giveth me shall come to me; and him that cometh to me I will in no wise cast out. 38For I came down from heaven, not to do mine own will, but the will of him that sent me. 39And this is the Father's will which hath sent me, that of all which he hath given me I should lose nothing, but should raise it up again at the last day. 40And this is the will of him that sent me, that every one which seeth the Son, and believeth on him, may have everlasting life: and I will raise him up at the last day. 41The Jews then murmured at him, because he said, I am the bread which came down from heaven. 42And they said, Is not this Jesus, the son of Joseph, whose father and mother we know? how is it then that he saith, I came down from heaven?

...

47Verily, verily, I say unto you, He that believeth on me hath everlasting life. 48I am that bread of life. John 6:32-48 KJV

The Messiah here presents a level of truth so profound that it completely perplexed the Jewish leaders.

> ^{66}*From that time many of his disciples went back, and walked no more with him.* ^{67}*Then said Jesus unto the twelve, Will ye also go away?* ^{68}*Then Simon Peter answered him, Lord, to whom shall we go? thou hast the words of eternal life.* ^{69}*And we believe and are sure that thou art that Christ, the Son of the living God. John 6:66-69 KJV*
>
> *Do you know Him? Or do you just know about him!*

REFLECTIONS ON JOHN 7

"NOT THIS TOWN"!

As Jesus walks around Galilee, he would not go to where the Jews where, because they sought to kill him. His brothers, attempted to convince him to go into town and show the people what he can do. Then comes one of the saddest text in scripture.

> *His brethren therefore said unto him, Depart hence, and go into Judaea, that thy disciples also may see the works that thou doest.* ^{4}*For there is no man that doeth anything in secret, and he himself seeketh to be known openly. If thou do these things, shew thyself to the world.* ^{5}*For neither did his brethren believe in him. John 7:4-5 KJV*

If thou do these things? Even his own brothers rejected Jesus. Not only did they not follow him, verse five says, they did not believe in him.

Many of us face this challenge every day. What do you do, and how does it affect you when the people closest to you do not support you? I have good news for situations like this. Look at Jesus's response!

> ^{6}*Then Jesus said unto them, My time is not yet come: but your time is alway ready. John 7:6 KJV*

Years ago a professor presented a charge to encourage his students. That charge still rings throughout the halls of the university's campus, and across the byways of life. It can still be heard! Go On, Go On, Go On, Go On, Go On, Go On, Go On, Go On, Go On, Go On, Go On, Go On, Go On, Go On, Go On, Go On!

REFLECTIONS ON JOHN 8

INVISIBLE IN PLAIN SIGHT

Sometimes the closer things are, the harder they are to see. If this is something you have experienced do not be alarmed. There is a medical explanation for it. It is called Hyperopia! What is it?

Hyperopia: Noun

A condition in which visual images come to a focus behind the retina of the eye and vision is better for distant than for near objects

Farsightedness, or **hyperopia**, as it is medically termed, is a vision condition in which distant objects can be seen clearly, but close ones do not come into proper focus.

This physical condition also explains the spiritual condition of the Jewish leadership. Jesus was well aware that signs and miracles was not the way to the heart of pride. Nevertheless, signs and miracles are a natural result of those that believe and trust in God. Therefore, wherever those who trust God for guidance and are obedient to His will, well miracles follow them. This truth was no different for Jesus. He could not help but meet every need that he saw. Jesus came to this darkened world to guide fallen man into harmony with the will of the Father. Moreover, by accepting God's guidance He allows the Holy Spirit to transform sinful man into a loving servant. Love cannot see a need and not supply it, it is impossible to be "Born Again" as Jesus described it to Nicodemus, and not supply a soul in need. One Christian writer put it this way "Christ lived to bless others".

Even those suffering from spiritual "Hyperopia", he came to bless. He did not pass by any needy soul as the woman caught in adultery soon experienced.

Jesus went unto the mount of Olives. ²And early in the morning he came again into the temple, and all the people came unto him; and he sat down, and taught them. ³And the scribes and Pharisees brought unto him a woman taken in adultery; and when they had set her in the midst, ⁴They say unto him, Master, this woman was taken in adultery, in the very act. ⁵Now Moses in the law commanded us, that such should be stoned: but what sayest thou? ⁶This they said, tempting him, that they might have to accuse him. But Jesus stooped down, and with his finger wrote on the ground, as though he heard them not. So when they continued asking him, he lifted up himself, and said unto them, He that is without sin among you, let him first cast a stone at her. ⁸And again he stooped down, and wrote on the ground. John 8:2-8 KJV

I can imagine Jesus writing on the ground, Tarik you were with her just yesterday, Habib you lay with her three days ago, Akeem you tried late last evening but your wife asked where you were going.

⁹And they which heard it, being convicted by their own conscience, went out one by one, beginning at the eldest, even unto the last: and Jesus was left alone, and the woman standing in the midst. ¹⁰When Jesus had lifted up himself, and saw none but the woman, he said unto her, Woman, where are those thine accusers? hath no man condemned thee? ¹¹She said, No man, Lord. And Jesus said unto her, Neither do I condemn thee: go, and sin no more. John 9:9-11 KJV

What a beautiful gesture: do you remember John 3:17-20

¹⁷For God sent not his Son into the world to condemn the world; but that the world through him might be saved. ¹⁸He that believeth on him is not condemned: but he that believeth not is condemned already, because he hath not believed in the name of the only begotten Son of God. ¹⁹And this is the condemnation, that light is come into the world, and men loved darkness rather than light, because their deeds were evil. ²⁰For every one that doeth evil hateth the light, neither cometh to the light, lest his deeds should be reproved. John 3:17-20 KJV

When Jesus stooped down to write on the ground He was not condemning those who were also guilty, He was exposing them to the same opportunity He was about to make available to the woman caught in the very act. What is the difference?

They left unrepentant, she left forgiven! There is that vision problem again "Hyperopia". It reminds me of the Three Stooges,

Curley cries out to Moe, "Moe I can't see I can't see!" Moe responds "What's wrong Curley?" Curley responds *"I got my eye's closed!"*

There it is again light, open your eyes and live!

REFLECTIONS ON JOHN 9

A GIFT OF BLINDNESS

And as Jesus passed by, he saw a man which was blind from his birth. ²And his disciples asked him, saying, Master, who did sin, this man, or his parents, that he was born blind? ³Jesus answered, Neither hath this man sinned, nor his parents: but that the works of God should be made manifest in him. ⁴I must work the works of him that sent me, while it is day: the night cometh, when no man can work. ⁵As long as I am in the world, I am the light of the world. ⁶When he had thus spoken, he spat on the ground, and made clay of the spittle, and he anointed the eyes of the blind man with the clay, ⁷And said unto him, Go, wash in the pool of Siloam, (which is by interpretation, Sent.) He went his way therefore, and washed, and came seeing. John 9:1-7 KJV

Most people who read this account of Jesus healing the man blind from birth, cannot seem to get over Jesus spitting on the ground.

Does that bother you too? Truth is you cannot make clay without salt and water. Anyone who knows basic chemistry understands this. Build a bridge: "Get over it"

Do you feel me pulling your leg? Its' an old cliché.

The bigger issue here is that once again, Jesus delivers a desperate soul, and the only concern among the spiritual leaders is well; maybe I should let them speak for themselves.

> *¹⁵Then again the Pharisees also asked him how he had received his sight. He said unto them, He put clay upon mine eyes, and I washed, and do see. ¹⁶Therefore said some of the Pharisees, This man is not of God, because he keepeth not the sabbath day. Others said, how can a man that is a sinner do such miracles? And there was a division among them. John 9:15-16 KJV*

Once again Jesus heals a poor degraded soul, and the only thing the religious leaders are concerned about is that the law was violated. This healing caused a division among the Pharisees; some clearly see the hand of God, while others see the law violated.

> *³⁰The man answered and said unto them, Why herein is a marvellous thing, that ye know not from whence he is, and yet he hath opened mine eyes. ³¹Now we know that God heareth not sinners: but if any man be a worshipper of God, and doeth his will, him he heareth. ³²Since the world began was it not heard that any man opened the eyes of one that was born blind. ³³If this man were not of God, he could do nothing. ³⁴They answered and said unto him, Thou wast altogether born in sins, and dost thou teach us? And they cast him out. John 9:30-34 KJV*

Here is another Equation for you

BL + BF = BFID

Blind leaders plus Blind Followers equal both falling into ditch

> *³⁹And Jesus said, For judgment I am come into this world, that they which see not might see; and that they which see might be made blind. John 9:39 KJV*

THIEVES, ROBBERS AND STONES OH MY!

> *Verily, verily, I say unto you, He that entereth not by the door into the sheepfold, but climbeth up some other way, the same is a thief and a robber. ²But he that entereth in by the door is the shepherd of the sheep. ³To him the porter openeth; and the sheep hear his voice: and he calleth his own sheep by name, and leadeth them out. ⁴And when he putteth forth his own sheep, he goeth before them, and the sheep follow him: for they know his voice. ⁵And a stranger will they not follow, but will flee from him: for they know not the voice of strangers. ⁶This parable spake Jesus unto them: but they understood not what things they were which he spake unto them. John 10:1-6 KJV*

Here Jesus uses a parable to convey a message of truth about himself. This parable also explains why some are able to see and receive and others receive nothing at all. Listen to Jesus's explanation.

> *Then said Jesus unto them again, Verily, verily, I say unto you, I am the door of the sheep. ⁸All that ever came before me are thieves and robbers: but the sheep did not hear them. ⁹I am the door: by me if any man enter in, he shall be saved, and shall go in and out, and find pasture. ¹⁰The thief cometh not, but for to steal, and to kill, and to destroy: I am come that they might have life, and that they might have it more abundantly. ¹¹I am the good shepherd: the good shepherd giveth his life for the sheep. John 10:8-11 KJV*

This passage is probably one of the most profound statements Jesus has made to this point in His public ministry. In verse eleven, Jesus publicly acknowledges that true leadership is sacrificial.

This truth is one of the most ignored realities in modern day leadership today. Why? Because self-sacrifice is not a human principle, it's divine! And you can't fake it. Once again, Jesus cuts to the heart of the matter.

¹⁴I am the good shepherd, and know my sheep, and am known of mine. ¹⁵As the Father knoweth me, even so know I the Father: and I lay down my life for the sheep. ¹⁶And other sheep I have, which are not of this fold: them also I must bring, and they shall hear my voice; and there shall be one fold, and one shepherd. John 10:14-16 KJV

Jesus has just separated himself from the Jewish leaders. And with this statement He has left the Pharisees exposed and vulnerable. If you don't believe me look at their response!

¹⁹There was a division therefore again among the Jews for these sayings. ²⁰And many of them said, He hath a devil, and is mad; why hear ye him? ²¹Others said, These are not the words of him that hath a devil. Can a devil open the eyes of the blind? ³¹Then the Jews took up stones again to stone him. John 10:19-21,31KJV

THIEVES AND ROBBERS AND STONES OH MY!

REFLECTIONS ON JOHN 11

TEARS NO FEARS

This chapter covers the next miracle that Jesus performed and the only one that made the master cry.

Now a certain man was sick, named Lazarus, of Bethany, the town of Mary and her sister Martha. ²(It was that Mary which anointed the Lord with ointment, and wiped his feet with her hair, whose brother Lazarus was sick.) ³Therefore his sisters sent unto him, saying, Lord, behold, he whom thou lovest is sick. ⁴When Jesus heard that, he said, This sickness is not unto death, but for the glory of God, that the Son of God might be glorified thereby. John 11:1-4 KJV

In this passage Jesus is about to do something very confusing, He delays his departure to attend to His sick friend, knowing that Lazarus is near death. WHY? Watch This!

Then after that saith he to his disciples, Let us go into Judaea again. ⁸His disciples say unto him, Master, the Jews of late

sought to stone thee; and goest thou thither again? ⁹Jesus answered, Are there not twelve hours in the day? If any man walk in the day, he stumbleth not, because he seeth the light of this world. ¹⁰But if a man walk in the night, he stumbleth, because there is no light in him.11 These things said he: and after that he saith unto them, Our friend Lazarus sleepeth; but I go, that I may awake him out of sleep. ¹²Then said his disciples, Lord, if he sleep, he shall do well. ¹³Howbeit Jesus spake of his death: but they thought that he had spoken of taking of rest in sleep. ¹⁴Then said Jesus unto them plainly, Lazarus is dead. ¹⁵And I am glad for your sakes that I was not there, to the intent ye may believe; nevertheless let us go unto him. John 11:7-15KJV

At this point Jesus admits that if he had been present with Lazarus while he was sick then he would not have died. Do you remember when John announced:

⁴In him was life; and the life was the light of men. John 1:4.KJV

Jesus is about to perform his greatest miracle and with this miracle, he will prove that death has no power in the presence of the life giver. What can bring tears to a resurrection and reunion? What is it that moves the Messiah to weep, knowing that he is about to reunite his friend Lazarus with his sisters, is it tears of joy. Did the outpouring of emotion by Mary and Martha move Jesus? What is it that causes Jesus to weep?

Jesus weeps as his eye's fall on the grieving Mary and Martha, Jesus weeps as he beholds the grieving family and friends of Lazarus, Jesus weeps as he sees through prophetic vision that many of the mourners were still going to plot with the Sanhedrin to kill him and Lazarus. Jesus weeps as he sees that their rejection of his ministry to them would result in the Roman army's siege on Jerusalem and in the siege, many of the mourners present would die. This scene is actually the "Turning Point" the point at which all of earthly history turns! Forever!

³⁶Then said the Jews, Behold how he loved him! ³⁷And some of them said, Could not this man, which opened the eyes of the blind, have caused that even this man should not have died? John 11:36-37 KJV

There it is, ridicule mixed with grief. Until this point in Jesus's ministry the Pharisees and Sadducees would spread rumors about the miracles Jesus performed in an attempt to discredit the healing. In fact the Sadducees held the belief that the resurrection of the just was not correct. This led them to preach that no one could or would ever be raised from the dead. What Jesus was about to do would forever discredit their religious teaching. After this one there would be no rumor, only determined rejection of the Messiah.

Jesus was about to prove his claim that he was dependent on His Father and that He and His Father were indeed in harmony. Do you remember Jesus delayed his departure for two days after receiving news of Lazarus illness? Jesus was intentional about His delay. He was not being insensitive. The home of Lazarus, Mary and Martha was a place where Jesus often went to rest and be refreshed from the cares of life. Do you realize that the Light of the world did not have a home on earth; Jesus had to depend on the kindness of friends just for a place to lay his head at night. Indeed Lazarus was one of Jesus's first disciples, and was one of His most adherent defenders.

Jesus knew that if he rushed to Lazarus's side during illness there would be no miracle resurrection, no opportunity for many to believe on Him and alternately no salvation for humanity. After all Jesus was born to provide that perfect sacrifice for fallen humanity.

³⁸Jesus therefore again groaning in himself cometh to the grave. It was a cave, and a stone lay upon it. ³⁹Jesus said, Take ye away the stone. Martha, the sister of him that was dead, saith unto him, Lord, by this time he stinketh: for he hath been dead four days. ⁴⁰Jesus saith unto her, Said I not unto thee, that, if thou wouldest believe, thou shouldest see the glory of God? ⁴¹Then they took away the stone from the place where the dead was laid. And Jesus lifted up his eyes, and said, Father, I thank thee that thou hast heard me. ⁴²And

I knew that thou hearest me always: but because of the people which stand by I said it, that they may believe that thou hast sent me. ⁴³And when he thus had spoken, he cried with a loud voice, Lazarus, come forth. ⁴⁴And he that was dead came forth, bound hand and foot with graveclothes: and his face was bound about with a napkin. Jesus saith unto them, Loose him, and let him go. ⁴⁵Then many of the Jews which came to Mary, and had seen the things which Jesus did, believed on him. ⁴⁶But some of them went their ways to the Pharisees, and told them what things Jesus had done. ⁴⁷Then gathered the chief priests and the Pharisees a council, and said, What do we? for this man doeth many miracles. ⁴⁸If we let him thus alone, all men will believe on him: and the Romans shall come and take away both our place and nation. ⁴⁹And one of them, named Caiaphas, being the high priest that same year, said unto them, Ye know nothing at all, ⁵⁰Nor consider that it is expedient for us, that one man should die for the people, and that the whole nation perish not. ⁵¹And this spake he not of himself: but being high priest that year, he prophesied that Jesus should die for that nation; ⁵²And not for that nation only, but that also he should gather together in one the children of God that were scattered abroad. ⁵³Then from that day forth they took counsel together for to put him to death. ⁵⁴Jesus therefore walked no more openly among the Jews; but went thence unto a country near to the wilderness, into a city called Ephraim, and there continued with his disciples. John 11:38-54 KJV.

There it is "Jesus Wept" over the rejection of His sacrifice for His beloved children. Do you remember the children's song,

"Jesus loves the little children, all the children of the world, red and yellow, black and white they are precious in His sight, Jesus loves the little children of the world"?

You thought it was only a children's song didn't you? It is actually a truth for all generations.

Mary and Martha cried for their dead brother, who would soon live again. Jesus wept for His disobedient children who because of their rejection of the life giver, would never live again!

There It Is Again! Light shining through the darkness!

REFLECTIONS ON JOHN 12

I TOLD YOU

John chapter twelve is filled with irony after one of the greatest miracles Jesus has performed to date. I said to date, because what Jesus is about to do next sends Satan and the fallen angels into an unbridled ecstasy, more on that later!

> **Then Jesus six days before the passover came to Bethany, where Lazarus was, which had been dead, whom he raised from the dead.** [2]*There they made him a supper; and Martha served: but Lazarus was one of them that sat at the table with him.* [3]*Then took Mary a pound of ointment of spikenard, very costly, and anointed the feet of Jesus, and wiped his feet with her hair: and the house was filled with the odour of the ointment.* [4]*Then saith one of his disciples, Judas Iscariot, Simon's son, which should betray him,* [5]*Why was not this ointment sold for three hundred pence, and given to the poor?* [6]*This he said, not that he cared for the poor; but because he was a thief, and had the bag, and bare what was put therein.* [7]*Then said Jesus, Let her alone: against the day of my burying hath she kept this.* [8]*For the poor always ye have with you; but me ye have not always.* [9]*Much people of the Jews therefore knew that he was there: and they came not for Jesus' sake only, but that they might see Lazarus also, whom he had raised from the dead.* [10]*But the chief priests consulted that they might put Lazarus also to death;* [11]*Because that by reason of him many of the Jews went away, and believed on Jesus. John 12:1-11KJV*

Just as predicted the resurrection of Lazarus indeed caused some to believe, but many to reject Christ. The temptation for many Jews was evident. The

Romans were an occupying force in Jerusalem and forcing subscription on the Jewish nation. Among the Jewish leaders and people, many hoped that one day the Messiah would come and deliver them from Roman oppression. Jesus had the qualities they hoped for; after all, He could turn water into wine. He could feed thousands with just a few rations, heal the sick and even raise the dead. With a miracle worker like Jesus, they could certainly defeat the mighty Romans. Instead of proclaiming himself King, he spoke in parables, resisted the Rabbi's authority and proclaimed a message that had nothing to do with defeating the Romans. It seemed that Jesus was in many regards coming against the nation of Israel. Indeed Jesus proclaimed:

> [31]*And Jesus answering said unto them, They that are whole need not a physician; but they that are sick.* [32]*I came not to call the righteous, but sinners to repentance. Luke 5; 31-32 KJV.*

Yes! Jesus was indeed a revolutionary, poised to deliver his children from bondage, the bondage of sin!

Just as in our day, many of the religious leaders miss the intent of the gospel. It is not about rules or laws or feast days or who's got the details right, it's about people lost in sin and those who are saved use every resource to save those who are lost!

REFLECTIONS ON JOHN 13

THE OPEN SECRET

Many private organizations have some sort of secret process by which only members can participate. Like the airlines industry, only members identified as gold or silver, platinum or even elite can expect to board an aircraft before anyone else is allowed to board. I sometimes watch in amazement as people jockey for position often discourteous to their fellow passengers. Occasionally I wish that I were able to remind everyone that they have an assigned seat and because of the legal contract between you and the airline (the ticket) we're all going to leave and arrive at the same time.

I get it, everyone is trying to get the overhead bin storage space before it's all gone, and that's worth fighting for right? NOPE!

What about the secret club that has an initiation procedure? Once you have been accepted they require you to do strange things that no one can ever see or know about with the exception of the members. They seem intent on keeping you out, or at least in minimizing the size of the membership.

That is what I love about Jesus, he's just the opposite, he's trying to include everyone. Look at this description of the place he is preparing for those who love him,

> *[10]And he carried me away in the spirit to a great and high mountain, and shewed me that great city, the holy Jerusalem, descending out of heaven from God, [11]Having the glory of God: and her light was like unto a stone most precious, even like a jasper stone, clear as crystal; [12]And had a wall great and high, and had twelve gates, and at the gates twelve angels, and names written thereon, which are the names of the twelve tribes of the children of Israel: [13]On the east three gates; on the north three gates; on the south three gates; and on the west three gates. Revelation 21: 10-13 KJV*

> *[25]And the gates of it shall not be shut at all by day... Revelation 21:25 KJV*

Wow! What a wonderful place, did you see in verse twelve the city has twelve gates and in verse twenty-five the gates are never shut. Sounds like Jesus is letting everyone in, a place of inclusion.

Jesus reminds us:

> *[34]A new commandment I give unto you, That ye love one another; as I have loved you, that ye also love one another. [35]By this shall all men know that ye are my disciples, if ye have love one to another. John 14:34-35 KJV*

There it is, out in the open, Jesus's command is Love, not dogma or creed or even that you have all the details correct!

> *[4]Love is patient and kind; love is not jealous or boastful; [5]it is not arrogant or rude. Love does not insist on its own way; it is not irritable or resentful; 6it does not rejoice at wrong, but rejoices in the right. [7]Love bears all things, believes all things, hopes all things, endures all things. 1 Corinthians 13:4-7 RSV*

It really is that simple! Try it today!

REFLECTIONS ON *JOHN 14*

"THE PROMISE OF THE UPS"

I remember the Y2K crisis! Y2K what is that? Actually, it really was not a crisis at all, just a perceived one. Here is what lead to the concern. The United States as the rest of the industrialized world had completely accepted the digital revolution over the industrial age. Computers made work faster more efficient less costly and more manageable. The miniaturization of devices reduced the size of computers from mammoth room sized machines to miniature desktop devices. With these changes came a demand for more computer programmers, storage space and many other adaptations that placed stress on the rapidly growing industry.

For example in the 1960's and 1970's one kilobyte of storage would cost as much as one hundred dollars ($100.00). That's right one kilobyte! Today no one cares about a kilobyte; we talk in terms of Terabytes. However, in the 60's and 70's programmers had to find ways to conserve storage space. Therefore, when computer engineers wrote complex computer programs, they used a two-digit code to represent the year, and left out the first two digits.

For instance when the year was represented in computer code it was simply "65" or "66" or "87" "88". As we got closer to the new millennium someone discovered that there might be a problem when the date changed from 1999 to 2000. The concern was that the computers would not know how to process the year "00" and that would cause the computer to stop processing information.

In the year 1999 almost every industrial, process depended on embedded microchips. If microchips stop working, everything would stop working. From refrigerators to factories cars to airplanes telephones to rocket ships. Almost everything interrupted, and none of the experts were sure that the chips would work, can you see the problem! No power and no idea how long this potential disruption would last. As we all waited for the clock to strike midnight and 1999 became the year 2000, relief as things kept on working as normal.

Can you imagine what would have happened if everything shut down. No you cannot it is almost unthinkable, because it has never happened before. The power to keep on working is something we take for granted.

Jesus was beginning to prepare his disciples for the time when he would no longer be with them ln person.

Let not your heart be troubled: ye believe in God, believe also in me. ²In my Father's house are many mansions: if it were not so, I would have told you. I go to prepare a place for you. ³And if I go and prepare a place for you, I will come again, and receive you unto myself; that where I am, there ye may be also. John 14:1-3 KJV

Jesus introduces a masterful stroke of genius; he reminds His disciples that He has an uninterruptible power supply that will be with them always.

¹⁵If ye love me, keep my commandments. ¹⁶And I will pray the Father, and he shall give you another Comforter, that he may abide with you for ever; ¹⁷Even the Spirit of truth; whom the world cannot receive, because it seeth him not, neither knoweth him: but ye know him; for he dwelleth with you, and shall be in you. ¹⁸I will not leave you comfortless: I will come to you. ¹⁹Yet a little while, and the world seeth me no more; but ye see me: because I live, ye shall live also.

²⁵These things have I spoken unto you, being yet present with you. ²⁶But the Comforter, which is the Holy Ghost, whom the Father will send in my name, he shall teach you all things, and bring all things to your remembrance, whatsoever I have said unto you. ²⁷Peace I leave with you, my peace I give unto you: not as the world giveth, give I unto you. Let not your heart be troubled, neither let it be afraid. John 14:15-19: 25-27 KJV

There it is a UPS, the "uninterruptable Power Supply".

The Holy Spirit directed by the Father, dispatched by the Son to those that obey Him and keeps His commandments and cannot be seen, heard or interrupted by the world. Uninterruptable communication, power and Comfort 24/7/365 forever!

What a plan, what a privilege what a savior!

Thank you Jesus for a UPS!

REFLECTIONS ON JOHN 15

THE BACKLASH

As Jesus continues to prepare His disciples for His death, he reminds them that His connection with them is like a vine and its branches.

> *I am the true vine, and my Father is the husbandman. [2]Every branch in me that beareth not fruit he taketh away: and every branch that beareth fruit, he purgeth it, that it may bring forth more fruit. [3]Now ye are clean through the word which I have spoken unto you. [4]Abide in me, and I in you. As the branch cannot bear fruit of itself, except it abide in the vine; no more can ye, except ye abide in me. [5]I am the vine, ye are the branches: He that abideth in me, and I in him, the same bringeth forth much fruit: for without me ye can do nothing. John 15: 1-5 KJV*

Jesus is teaching here is a practical lesson for His disciples. Soon they will no longer be able to see Jesus physically, or walk or touch Him. So they must understand the way to communicate with him is through His Spirit. Jesus's words to abide in me and I will abide in you is the key to being productive and producing fruit in the physical absence of their master.

> *[7]If ye abide in me, and my words abide in you, ye shall ask what ye will, and it shall be done unto you.8 Herein is my Father glorified, that ye bear much fruit; so shall ye be my disciples. [9]As the Father hath loved me, so have I loved you: continue ye in my love. [10]If ye keep my commandments, ye shall abide in my love; even as I have kept my Father's commandments, and abide in his love. [11]These things have I spoken unto you, that my joy might remain in you, and that your joy might be full. [12]This is my commandment, That ye love one another, as I have loved you. [13]Greater love hath no man*

than this, that a man lay down his life for his friends. [14]Ye are my friends, if ye do whatsoever I command you.

John 15:7-14 KJV

Once again, Jesus emphasizes the power and importance of Love.

This kind of love is not attainable by human effort; it's the gift of God. This gift allows the receiver to accomplish what Jesus describes as the litmus test of discipleship, Spirit lead disciples who love each other. This love is not an emotion it is not a feeling,

It is a highly motivated divine principal.

Divine because it comes from God by His Spirit. Motivated by the believer's obedience to Christ commandment. Principled because of the power of the indwelling Christ through His Spirit that gives the believer the power to love unconditionally.

[17]These things I command you, that ye love one another. [18]If the world hate you, ye know that it hated me before it hated you. [19]If ye were of the world, the world would love his own: but because ye are not of the world, but I have chosen you out of the world, therefore the world hateth you. [20]Remember the word that I said unto you, The servant is not greater than his lord. If they have persecuted me, they will also persecute you; if they have kept my saying, they will keep yours also. [21]But all these things will they do unto you for my name's sake, because they know not him that sent me. [22]If I had not come and spoken unto them, they had not had sin: but now they have no cloak for their sin [23]He that hateth me hateth my Father also. [24]If I had not done among them the works which none other man did, they had not had sin: but now have they both seen and hated both me and my Father. [25]But this cometh to pass, that the word might be fulfilled that is written in their law, They hated me without a cause. [26]But when the Comforter is come, whom I will send unto you from the Father, even the Spirit of truth, which proceedeth from the Father, he shall testify of me: John 15: 17-26 KJV

How ironic, Jesus fed them healed them saved them and still He loves them. That is our mission, that's our aim that's our Savior!

REFLECTIONS ON JOHN 16 & 17

"PREPARATION FOR THE COMING CRISIS"

> [7]*Nevertheless I tell you the truth; It is expedient for you that I go away: for if I go not away, the Comforter will not come unto you; but if I depart, I will send him unto you.* [8]*And when he is come, he will reprove the world of sin, and of righteousness, and of judgment:* [9]*Of sin, because they believe not on me;* [10]*Of righteousness, because I go to my Father, and ye see me no more;* [11]*Of judgment, because the prince of this world is judged.* [12]*I have yet many things to say unto you, but ye cannot bear them now.* [13]*Howbeit when he, the Spirit of truth, is come, he will guide you into all truth: for he shall not speak of himself; but whatsoever he shall hear, that shall he speak: and he will shew you things to come.* [14]*He shall glorify me: for he shall receive of mine, and shall shew it unto you.*
> *John 16:7-14 KJV*

Here is where I inform you that the objects on the screen may appear larger than they actually are, but they are not! This is probably the most misunderstood if not outright ignored truth in scripture! Look at the words of Jesus again!

> Verse 8: *And when he is come, he will reprove the world of sin, and of righteousness, and of judgment:*

In this verse Jesus clearly explains, when the Holy Spirit comes it is His responsibility to convince the world that they are in violation of Gods law. In addition, the Spirit of God will show the sinner what is right and that the person who continues in sin will be judged according to Gods law. So what is the takeaway here?

First, it is not Gods plan that men would convict their fellow men of sin. God's design is that men would become His witnesses and testify on behalf of His goodness. Second, it is the Holy Spirit's job to provide the power for sinful man to live above the temptation of sin and finally the Spirit of God convinces the sinner that judgement is coming.

This is why Jesus is explaining to His disciples that He must go away. Jesus is limited by His humanity, He is not omnipresent, he cannot be everywhere at the same time.

The Holy Spirit is omnipresent! He can be wherever God's children have need at an instant. Somebody shouted Hallelujah!

Jesus continues to explain in verse 13:

Howbeit when he, the Spirit of truth, is come, he will guide you into all truth: for he shall not speak of himself; but whatsoever he shall hear, that shall he speak: and he will shew you things to come.

Herein lies the key to a proliferation of beliefs and dogmas and customs and religions and confusion. Jesus clearly teaches that it is the Holy Spirit that leads the believer into what is truth. Can you see it? Jesus followed the plan of His Father so patiently that He was able to perform miracles, setting His children free from the power of their nature to sin. That is the power of the Holy Spirit, Jesus declared that He did nothing of himself it was the power of the Father through Him to us.

Since Jesus must leave, He promises not to leave His children without a comforter. In addition, this is how God's plan is accomplished in the earth. The Holy Spirit, the uninterrupted source of power for Gods children to overcome their nature to sin.

What would our world be like if men would submit to the guidance of God's Holy Spirit? You are right it would be Heaven!

So you have sorrow now, but I will see you again and your hearts will rejoice, and no one will take your joy from you. 23 In that day you will ask nothing of me. Truly, truly, I say to you, if you ask anything of the Father, he will give it to you in my name. 24 Hitherto you have asked nothing in my name; ask, and you will receive, that your joy may be full. John 16:22-24 RSV

In life sorrow is inevitable, people convicted to live according to Gods plan will often come into conflict with people determined to live according to their own lust. You do not have to confront the sinner with his error; your obedient life is an affront to him.

Your presence alone is a constant reminder of the sinner's condition. Therefore, Jesus continues to prepare and encourage His disciples.

> [33]*I have said this to you, that in me you may have peace. In the world you have tribulation; but be of good cheer, I have overcome the world." John 16:33 KJV*

Here Jesus prays to His Father for His disciples; listen to how He speaks to His Father.

> *I have given them thy word; and the world has hated them because they are not of the world, even as I am not of the world. 15 I do not pray that thou shouldst take them out of the world, but that thou shouldst keep them from the evil one.[a] 16 They are not of the world, even as I am not of the world. 17 Sanctify them in the truth; thy word is truth. John 17:14-17 KJV*

The word Jesus uses here is "sanctify" them, what does He mean by sanctify? It is important to note, the Jewish concept of the word "sanctify" is different from the modern concept.

Here is how! The word Jesus uses here is the Hebrew word "kodesh" which literally means holiness. Jesus is asking His Father to set His disciples apart so that they can serve a holy purpose.

In modern times Jesus request from His Father is often interpreted, make them holy with special powers and worthy of veneration. Do you see the difference? Jesus is asking for the power to serve, men today believe their position is the right to be served.

Jesus literally says, Father set my disciples apart from the world so that they can be used to serve a holy purpose. Moreover, set them apart through your word because your word is the truth!

And the glory which thou gavest me I have given them; that they may be one, even as we are one: John 17:22 KJV

Here is a new equation for you!

H x O = U

Holiness produces Oneness and Oneness creates Unity

REFLECTIONS ON JOHN 18-19

WHAT YA' LOOKIN FOR

The time that Jesus was preparing His disciples for had come.

Jesus went into a familiar garden to pray. Judas the one that would betray Jesus also knew this place well and suddenly appeared with armed men to take Jesus away.

> *Jesus therefore, knowing all things that should come upon him, went forth, and said unto them, Whom seek ye? ⁵They answered him, Jesus of Nazareth. Jesus saith unto them, I am he. And Judas also, which betrayed him, stood with them. ⁶As soon then as he had said unto them, I am he, they went backward, and fell to the ground. ⁷Then asked he them again, Whom seek ye? And they said, Jesus of Nazareth. ⁸Jesus answered, I have told you that I am he: if therefore ye seek me, let these go their way: ⁹That the saying might be fulfilled, which he spake, Of them which thou gavest me have I lost none. John 18:4-9 KJV*

Even in His distress, Jesus thought about the safety of His disciples.

> *Then Simon Peter having a sword drew it, and smote the high priest's servant, and cut off his right ear. The servant's name was Malchus. ¹¹Then said Jesus unto Peter, Put up thy sword into the sheath: the cup which my Father hath given me, shall I not drink it? ¹²Then the band and the captain and officers of the Jews took Jesus, and bound him, ¹³And led him away to Annas first; for he was father in law to Caiaphas, which was the high priest that same year. ¹⁴Now Caiaphas was he, which*

gave counsel to the Jews, that it was expedient that one man should die for the people. John 18:10-14 KJV

The gentle Jesus allowed himself to be taken. He did not resist but bore insult patiently. He endured the mockery and disdain of the Jewish leaders yet he did not resist.

> *Then Pilate therefore took Jesus, and scourged him. ²And the soldiers platted a crown of thorns, and put it on his head, and they put on him a purple robe, ³And said, Hail, King of the Jews! and they smote him with their hands. ⁴Pilate therefore went forth again, and saith unto them, Behold, I bring him forth to you, that ye may know that I find no fault in him. ⁵Then came Jesus forth, wearing the crown of thorns, and the purple robe. And Pilate saith unto them, Behold the man! ⁶When the chief priests therefore and officers saw him, they cried out, saying, Crucify him, crucify him. Pilate saith unto them, Take ye him, and crucify him: for I find no fault in him. ⁷The Jews answered him, We have a law, and by our law he ought to die, because he made himself the Son of God. John 19:1-7 KJV*

Jesus was fulfilling prophecy right before the people's eyes. Although they were aquatinted with the scriptures, they were blinded but their selfish ambitions. Isaiah's prophecy was fulfilled in their presence that day and they never saw it coming.

> *He is despised and rejected of men; a man of sorrows, and acquainted with grief: and we hid as it were our faces from him; he was despised, and we esteemed him not. Isaiah 53:3 KJV*

> *But he was wounded for our transgressions, he was bruised for our iniquities: the chastisement of our peace was upon him; and with his stripes we are healed. ⁶All we like sheep have gone astray; we have turned every one to his own way; and the Lord hath laid on him the iniquity of us all. Isaiah 53: 5-6 KJV*

He was oppressed, and he was afflicted, yet he opened not his mouth: he is brought as a lamb to the slaughter, and as a sheep before her shearers is dumb, so he openeth not his mouth. Isaiah 53:7 KJV

He was in the world, and the world was made by him, and the world knew him not. ¹¹He came unto his own, and his own received him not. John 1:11 KJV

But they cried out, Away with him, away with him, crucify him. Pilate saith unto them, Shall I crucify your King? The chief priests answered, We have no king but Caesar. John 19:15 KJV

I have no words!

REFLECTIONS ON JOHN 20-21

MISSION ACCOMPLISHED

It appeared as though what Jesus was saying was somewhat unclear if not a little delusional when He declared, destroy this temple and I will raise it up again in three days.

Now in the place where he was crucified there was a garden; and in the garden a new sepulchre, wherein was never man yet laid. ⁴²There laid they Jesus therefore because of the Jews' preparation day; for the sepulchre was nigh at hand. John 19:42-43 KJV

This text places a reference for the day and timeframe that Jesus died. "The Jews preparation day" is Friday the day before Saturday the Sabbath.

The first day of the week cometh Mary Magdalene early, when it was yet dark, unto the sepulchre, and seeth the stone taken away from the sepulchre. John 20:1 KJV

Even in death Jesus was accurate and obedient to His word. Indeed Christ was raised in three days, he died Friday afternoon, stayed in the tomb Saturday and rose early Sunday morning, are you shouting yet!

Then she runneth, and cometh to Simon Peter, and to the other disciple, whom Jesus loved, and saith unto them, They have taken away the Lord out of the sepulchre, and we know not where they have laid him. ³Peter therefore went forth, and that other disciple, and came to the sepulchre. ⁴So they ran both together: and the other disciple did outrun Peter, and came first to the sepulchre. ⁵And he stooping down, and looking in, saw the linen clothes lying; yet went he not in. ⁶Then cometh Simon Peter following him, and went into the sepulchre, and seeth the linen clothes lie, ⁷And the napkin, that was about his head, not lying with the linen clothes, but wrapped together in a place by itself. ⁸Then went in also that other disciple, which came first to the sepulchre, and he saw, and believed. ⁹For as yet they knew not the scripture, that he must rise again from the dead. ¹⁰Then the disciples went away again unto their own home.

But Mary stood without at the sepulchre weeping: and as she wept, she stooped down, and looked into the sepulchre, ¹²And seeth two angels in white sitting, the one at the head, and the other at the feet, where the body of Jesus had lain. ¹³And they say unto her, Woman, why weepest thou? She saith unto them, Because they have taken away my Lord, and I know not where they have laid him. ¹⁴And when she had thus said, she turned herself back, and saw Jesus standing, and knew not that it was Jesus. John 20:2-14 KJV

This is a long passage shared with you. I hope you can feel the tension in each word in every scene. Did you notice that when Mary ran to tell Peter and that other disciple who Jesus loved that Jesus was not in the tomb, Mary said they have taken him away? Did you also notice after the disciples looked in the tomb for themselves they just went back home. Strange behavior isn't it? Verse nine sums it up,

For as yet they knew not the scripture, that he must rise again from the dead. John 20:9 KJV

For three and a half years, the disciples hung on every word of Jesus and still they did not understand. All the miracles all the hard times, but watching their master give up without a struggle.

Well that was more than they could comprehend.

The disciples were hiding or at least keeping a low profile for fear they would be next. They were all on board when the wine was flowing and the fish and loves were multiplying, they were kind of like celebrities when Jesus was healing the blind and raising the dead.

Now their leader their master was dead and they were afraid for their own lives. Actually the Sanhedrin was also afraid, they considered what they would do if Jesus's disciples would come and steal his body away so that his claim that he would rise again would be realized. So the Jews convinced Pilate to place guards at the tomb to prevent the disciples from stealing Jesus's body and claiming that he had indeed risen from the dead. How ironic that the Jewish religious leaders remembered Jesus's words that he would rise again but the disciples did not.

Jesus even reminded them

"And ye now therefore have sorrow: but I will see you again, and your heart shall rejoice, and your joy no man taketh from you. John 16:22 KJV

However, the disciples were disappointed, for they like everyone else believed Jesus was going to reestablish the Jewish nation and remove the Romans from their homeland. Mystery of mysteries and now everyone was disappointed. The Jewish leaders had succeeded in killing Jesus by convincing the Romans to do it for them and now they cannot produce a body.

Jesus's disciples were disappointed for the miracle worker was dead, so now they would have to go back to fishing if they could somehow stay alive themselves. Then comes Jesus!

Jesus saith unto her, Woman, why weepest thou? whom seekest thou? She, supposing him to be the gardener, saith unto him, Sir, if thou have borne him hence, tell me where thou hast laid him, and I will take him away. [16] Jesus saith unto her, Mary. She turned herself, and saith unto him, Rabboni; which is to say, Master. [17] Jesus saith unto her, Touch me not; for I am not yet ascended to my Father: but go to my brethren, and say unto them, I ascend unto my Father, and your Father; and to my God, and your God. [18]Mary Magdalene came and told the disciples that she had seen the Lord, and that he had spoken these things unto her. [19]Then the same day at evening, being the first day of the week, when the doors were shut where the disciples were assembled for fear of the Jews, came Jesus and stood in the midst, and saith unto them, Peace be unto you. [20]And when he had so said, he shewed unto them his hands and his side. Then were the disciples glad, when they saw the Lord. [21]Then said Jesus to them again, Peace be unto you: as my Father hath sent me, even so send I you. [22]And when he had said this, he breathed on them, and saith unto them, Receive ye the Holy Ghost: John 20:15-22 KJV

And many other signs truly did Jesus in the presence of his disciples, which are not written in this book:

[31]But these are written, that ye might believe that Jesus is the Christ, the Son of God; and that believing ye might have life through his name. John 20: 30-31 KJV.

After these things Jesus shewed himself again to the disciples at the sea of Tiberias; and on this wise shewed he himself.

This is now the third time that Jesus shewed himself to his disciples, after that he was risen from the dead.

[15]So when they had dined, Jesus saith to Simon Peter, Simon, son of Jonas, lovest thou me more than these? He saith unto him, Yea, Lord; thou knowest that I love thee. He saith unto him, Feed my lambs. [16]He saith to him again the second time, Simon, son of Jonas, lovest thou me? He saith unto him, Yea, Lord; thou knowest that I love thee. He saith unto him, Feed my sheep. [17]He saith unto him the third time, Simon, son of Jonas, lovest thou me? Peter was grieved because he said unto him the third time, Lovest thou me? And he said unto him,

Lord, thou knowest all things; thou knowest that I love thee.
Jesus saith unto him, Feed my sheep. John 21:15-17 KJV

The disciple's disappointment over the loss of the Messiah caused them to return to what they were doing before Jesus called them to his side. However, what they were about to receive would change everything. Do you remember earlier I mentioned that when Jesus repeats himself look out for an emphatic revelation. Here Jesus says to Peter 3 times "Feed My Sheep ". Do you remember how many times Peter denied that he knew Jesus while in Pilate's judgement hall? Yes, 3 times, Peter denied the Lord.

Before we become too critical of the disciples, consider what we have read. The truth is, what is written in scripture is recorded for our benefit. When we look at the disciples, weak, confused and afraid, we are looking at ourselves. They witnessed His ministry but could not comprehend it all. We read their account of what happened and still we do not believe. I believe it all comes down to *John 20:22*

> *²²And when he had said this, he breathed on them, and saith unto them, Receive ye the Holy Ghost:*

Are you willing to receive His Spirit today?

> *This is the disciple which testifieth of these things, and wrote these things: and we know that his testimony is true.25 And there are also many other things which Jesus did, the which, if they should be written every one, I suppose that even the world itself could not contain the books that should be written. Amen. John 21:24-25 KJV*

CONCLUSION

Revelation is not old, stale, decayed, outdated and irrelevant. As God gave fresh manna daily to his children centuries ago in the wilderness, so He gives fresh revelation related to the diligent study His Word in these times. This revelation is not limited a select group of people. It is available to all who faithfully study and obey God's Word. That means you too can have and share Fresh Manna! Our concluding encouragement is to keep studying the Bible. Keep applying what you discover in study to your personal life. Keep sharing the revelations you gain from your study. This wonderful, life enhancing, soul saving, satisfying Bread of life will keep you safe and productive in this present wilderness, while sustaining you on your journey to the heavenly promise land. God bless you and may the Holy Spirit guide you. Amen!